SECOND FOUNDING

SECOND FOUNDING

New York City, Reconstruction, and the Making of American Democracy

DAVID QUIGLEY

HILL AND WANG

A division of Farrar, Straus and Giroux

New York

A division of Farrar, Straus and Giroux
19 Union Square West, New York 10003

Copyright © 2004 by David Quigley
Distributed in Canada by Douglas & McIntyre Ltd.
Printed in the United States of America
First edition, 2004

Library of Congress Cataloging-in-Publication Data
Quigley, David, 1966–
    Second founding : New York City, Reconstruction, and the making of
American democracy / by David Quigley.— 1st ed.
        p.   cm.
Includes bibliographical references (p.   ).
    ISBN 0-8090-8514-3 (alk. paper)
    1. Reconstruction—New York (State)—New York.   2. New York
(N.Y.)—History—1865–1898.   3. New York (N.Y.)—Politics and govern-
ment—To 1898.   4. Democracy—New York (State)—New York—His-
tory—19th century.   5. New York (N.Y.)—Race relations.   I. Title.

    F128.47.Q54 2004
    974.7′1041—dc21

                                                            2003012610

Designed by Jonathan D. Lippincott

www.fsgbooks.com

1   3   5   7   9   10   8   6   4   2

To Megan

CONTENTS

PREFACE

The unending tragedy of Reconstruction is the utter inability of the American mind to grasp its real significance, its national and world-wide implications.   —W. E. B. Du Bois[1]

This is a book about modern America at its founding moment, the years after the Civil War. Reconstruction, more than any other event in the nation's past, determined just what kind of politics Americans would have. Back in 1787, America's first founding had produced a constitution profoundly skeptical of democracy. James Madison and his coauthors in Philadelphia left undecided fundamental questions of slavery and freedom. All that would change in the 1860s and 1870s. Decided at this second founding were the rules of the democratic game. Though lasting only a few short years, Reconstruction involved countless Americans fighting over who would be able to play in that game, and on whose terms. A century and a quarter later, the democracy that emerged at Reconstruction's end remains our inheritance.[2]

To be sure, the post–Civil War era stands as a most peculiar founding. It was as much about renouncing the slave republic's legacies as it was an attempt to establish that rare polity, an interracial democracy. This dialectic of tearing down and rebuilding lies at the conflicted heart of Reconstruction. Slavery had been driven off the American stage, and North and South, East and West, Americans for the first time struggled over the establishment of a democracy open to all races. Adding to the modernity of this project was the fact that the term *democracy* itself was no longer anathema, as it had been a century earlier. By 1865, democracy stood as both national ideal and the nation's institutional arrangements most in need of reconstruction.

The second founding, with its lack of a clearly defined center and its heterogeneous character, marks the advent of the modern age in American politics. Early national illustrations of the Philadelphia Convention—depicting elite white men meeting in one city, neatly tucked away from public view—capture well the homogeneity of America's first founders. Four score years later, Reconstruction could not be similarly contained; the debate over the second founding raged in the urban North, the rural South, and on to the frontiers of the West. And the second founders reflected the ascendant pluralistic America of the late nineteenth century. Frederick Douglass and Elizabeth Cady Stanton were but two of the leading public figures of the day. The reconstruction of democracy occasioned an unprecedentedly expansive conversation, reflecting an inclusiveness unthinkable in Madison's day.

Decentered, pluralistic, and deeply divided, the second founding speaks directly to contemporary Americans and our politics. In the 1860s and 1870s, this nation for the first time struggled over the substance of an industrializing, urbanizing, and, most important, *interracial* democracy. The original founding had either tragically mishandled or been able to avoid issues of race relations, industrial capitalism, and city life. After the Civil War, at the second founding, Americans confronted these concerns through a historic, wide-ranging struggle over the meanings, practices, and possibilities of democracy.

It was in New York City that this historic reconstruction of democracy realized its fullest dimensions. On the streets of postwar Manhattan, the accelerating forces of economic change, urbanization, and racial revolution all converged and left American democracy forever transformed. As a result, the city's history affords the best opportunity for viewing Reconstruction's far-ranging impact on the development of democratic politics. That history is necessarily a national story, revealing American democracy in the process of remaking itself. Only by grasping what happened in New York City in these years can we come to understand Reconstruction's "national and worldwide implications."[3]

The white supremacist traditions of the nation's leading city mitigated against any far-reaching revision of America's racial order. The hellish racial violence of the Draft Riots of July 1863, in which over one hundred Manhattanites were killed, were but the most extreme manifestation of an abiding antiblack rage among white New Yorkers. Two Manhattan Democrats went so far as to vote in 1865 against the Thirteenth Amendment, which forever abolished slavery in the United States. Metropolitan politicians placed limits on the possibilities of Republicans' Reconstruction program at every turn. Yet change did occur in the postwar years; a new America—and a new New York—took shape. The era's amendments to the federal Constitution required New Yorkers to practice a politics far removed from their antebellum traditions of whites-only democracy. The federal government's expanded powers translated into a new force to be reckoned with in Manhattan's neighborhoods. New languages and practices of pubic life took root in the city in the decade and a half after the Civil War.

And particular features of the city rendered its influence pivotal in national life during Reconstruction. As the central site of various national intellectual, political, and economic networks, New York exerted vast power in postbellum America. The city emerged by the 1860s as the nation's preeminent cultural center. New York publishers now dominated the production of reading material for both elite and mass audiences. As local newspapers influenced coverage in dailies across the continent, metropolitan editors and writers shaped national discussions throughout the postwar years. In the political realm, the local Democratic Party—led by Tammany Hall—emerged as the headquarters of the opposition during Republican Reconstruction. Samuel J. Tilden and other New York Democrats managed to direct their party's strategy while they succeeded at forging long-lasting ties between the local party and the emerging Solid South. The site of numerous conventions of political parties and reform organizations, Manhattan consolidated its position as a central place of American public life.

Economically, the postwar years witnessed the ever-increasing leadership of New York financiers and the rise of metropolitan industrialists. During this early Gilded Age, the "robber barons"—the powerful class of wealthy postbellum Americans—came together in Manhattan's elite neighborhoods. These New Yorkers defined themselves apart from their fellow city residents and from many of their fellow Americans.[4] At the same time, mounting business-class confidence and the economic crises of the 1870s gave rise to a militant working-class movement in the city. New Yorkers, as they battled each other, were shaping modern Americans' understanding of society.

Those present at the second founding in New York included black activists, Tammany Democrats, bourgeois reformers, liberal publicists, women's suffrage leaders, and trade unionists. While pursuing very different political programs, all agreed that the postbellum years offered a rare opportunity to resolve the nation's enduring dilemmas. The African American minister Henry Highland Garnet, the charity reformer Josephine Shaw Lowell, the labor journalist John Swinton among countless other New Yorkers helped frame the new political order that emerged after the Civil War. These activists-publicists-intellectuals built new urban networks, linking religious and secular organizations with journalistic outlets and the city's political parties.

Because the second founding involved so many New Yorkers and encompassed such a vast terrain, this narrative, by necessity, travels beyond the Hudson and East Rivers. Much of the most heated debate over democratic life took place outside of Manhattan, whether up in Albany or within the halls of Congress in Washington, D.C. More than other histories of New York City, this narrative highlights the conflicted relationship between the metropolis and the nation.[5] Reconstruction was also a moment when Americans paid a great deal of attention to events outside of the United States. The Paris Commune, the failed revolutionary movement of the spring of 1871 in whose violent suppression at least twenty thousand French citizens were killed, was a local Manhattan obsession for much of the rest of the decade, helping shape the political consciousness of many New Yorkers at the dawn of the Gilded Age. Leading political thinkers and public figures like Samuel J. Tilden and John Swinton took extended trips overseas to observe Third Republic France and learn from England in the Age of Gladstone. The era of the American Civil War and Reconstruction marked a new stage in the nation's relationship with western Europe; New Yorkers forged the ties and crafted the languages that framed the increasingly transatlantic intellectual and political worlds of the late nineteenth century.

The tendencies within American culture that came to a head in New York in the years after the Civil War gave shape to politics for the late nineteenth century as well as for our own time. The enduring dilemmas of modern democracy were born, as Manhattanites confronted questions of urban politics and social justice. Slavery was abolished, but New York City, the birthplace of Jim Crow and the site of the 1863 Draft Riots, confronted the intertwined challenges of race and class in the late 1860s and 1870s and began an ongoing experiment in interracial urban life. The late 1860s gave rise to a metropolitan labor movement increasingly committed to racial exclusion and a politics of "the white workingman's democracy." In these years, the black freedom struggle resumed in Manhattan but faced abundant white working-class antipathy. In that decade, many New Yorkers—both black and white— appropriated the Fourteenth Amendment as the last refuge of the scorned and oppressed. The remaking of racial and class relations in the postwar decade gave way in time to the most violent period of class conflict in American history. The limitations and the possibilities of our own public life are, to a considerable degree, rooted in the compromises reached in Manhattan in the 1870s as much as those of the rural South.

The reconstruction of democracy in New York City further resulted in a radical redefinition of reform in urban America. A new generation of reformers replaced antebellum feminism and abolitionist antiracism with a conservative movement dedicated to the defense of class values and a politics of retrenchment. Central to this new model of urban reform was the privileging of the special rights of taxpayers. Bourgeois New Yorkers came to articulate a corporate understanding of public life; government was to be run as an efficient business enterprise, apart from the "dangers of democracy."

To understand this urban story of the second founding of American politics is to grasp the need for a reassessment of New York's place in American history. For too long, New Yorkers and non–New Yorkers alike have been confused about the relationship between the city and national politics. Manhattan natives tend to imagine their city as an oasis of cosmopolitan liberalism, standing apart from the rest of the United States. Many other Americans view New York as outside of the nation's political mainstream, as home either to a radical fringe or to a scheming cabal of elitists. Both sides are wrong. New York City, properly understood, has long been central to the making and remaking of democracy in America.

In the years after the Civil War, the city helped determine the course of Reconstruction nationally and arrived at the earliest fully modern, if compromised, understanding of democratic life. The arguments, arrangements, and assumptions of that understanding have framed our public life for well over a century. As long as Americans neglect the second founding's legacies, America will remain a nation asleep to the full dimensions of its most important political drama, blind to its best democratic possibilities, incapable of reconstructing anew.

PART ONE

DEMOCRATIC VISTAS

(1863–1866)

1

AFTER THE RIOTS

Friday, July 17, 1863

At last, the long, hot week of Manhattan's rage seemed to
have passed.

New Yorkers woke up that Friday morning to evidence of
a city gone mad. The metropolitan dailies continued to spill
forth news of previously unimaginable atrocities: black bodies
lynched, mobs setting upon lone women, the unspeakable
condition of bodies brought to the city morgue. Around Manhattan Island, over five thousand Union army soldiers now
maintained order, most of them having only recently arrived
from the Gettysburg theater of the war. Wall Street was an
armed fortress, as troops massed near the New York Stock Exchange and federal gunboats lay off the battery. The Manhattan waterfront was a no-man's-land, having been the site
of some of the worst violence over the previous four days.
Around the city, bodies of lynched black men were taken
down and buried. The Colored Orphan's Asylum on Fifth Avenue, now a ruin, gave evidence of the savagery that sim-
mered within the heart of the nation's metropolis. The week
of hellish riot left visible a scarred cityscape.

The New York City Draft Riots stand as the worst outbreak of mob violence in the history of American cities. At
least one hundred died in the riots. Inspired initially by anger
at the first draft in American history, masses of white Manhattanites vented their rage all week long at a range of targets.
Symbols of Republican power and elite strongholds were destroyed. The most intense and sustained violence, however,
was directed at the city's dwindling black community. The
African American neighborhood near Sullivan and Thompson
Streets lay under siege for two days. Bellevue Hospital filled
with seriously injured black New Yorkers ranging from children to the elderly. Scores of African American men, women,
and children huddled at the Eighth Precinct Station House,
desperate for protection from the rioters.[1]

New York's second founding would begin amid these horrors, a world of urban devastation with few parallels in American history. The wounds of July 1863 continued to haunt the
city's politics and culture for decades. African American vulnerability to explosive white mob violence has rarely been
clearer in the nation's history. The reconstruction of New York
City—and the nation—would forever remain in the long
shadows of the draft riots.

Thousands of Manhattan blacks abandoned the city in the
aftermath of July's violence. As the riot week came to an end,
mob brutality initiated a decline in the city's black population
that would last for the remainder of the decade. The African
American community in New York City would fall by half
during the 1860s, declining by five thousand. As the Merchants' Committee for the Relief of Colored People Suffering
from the Late Riots reported, "these people had been forced
to take refuge on Blackwell's Island, at police stations, on the
outskirts of the city, in the swamps and woods back of Bergen,

New Jersey, at Weeksville, and in the barns and out-houses of the farmers of Long Island and Morrisania."[2]

Federal troops encamped around the city. Where the local police force had failed, with the riots dragging on for days, it was now up to General Meade's men to restore order. Thousands of Union army soldiers controlled major thoroughfares and kept the peace in the city's public squares. That these wartime troops were available at all was fortunate. Lee's recent retreat south across the Potomac freed the men of the 152nd New York Volunteers, the 74th Regiment of the New York National Guard, and the 26th Michigan Volunteers to occupy the city.

The previous seventy-two hours of mob violence still stands as the worst incident of civil unrest in American history. After congressional enactment in March of the Conscription Act of 1863, the first draft in the nation's history had begun on Saturday, July 11. Violence began in earnest on Monday the thirteenth and boiled over through Wednesday the fifteenth. Sporadic crowd violence continued through Thursday afternoon of the sixteenth.

As New Yorkers went about their business that Friday morning, the week's rioting seemed to be ending. Mayor Opdyke felt secure enough to issue a proclamation declaring the riots officially over. The conservative Republican announced that "the riotous assemblages have been dispersed. Business is running in its usual channels."[3] The city's working women and men made their way through now-wartorn streets and squares. The first concrete steps in the city's long reconstruction required thousands of men to rebuild damaged rail lines and to reconnect sabotaged telegraph lines.

Postriot Manhattan—a city of looted shops, burned-down orphanages, and lynched black bodies—was long haunted by memories of July 1863. In the riots' immediate wake, New Yorkers struggled to make sense of the violence, the ongoing Civil War, and the city's place in a reconstructed Union. As Iver Bernstein, author of the definitive study of the draft riots and their contexts, argues, those who lived through the events of July 1863 collectively experienced a loss of bearings, unable to make sense of "a violent style of social and political resistance that was, at least in the American context, entirely new."[4] The second founding in Manhattan was, to a considerable extent, an attempt to come to terms with this profoundly new style of urban politics.

As the week's violence abated, countless rumors swept through the city's neighborhoods. Newspapers printed reports of gangs of Confederate agents living in various Manhattan boardinghouses and tenements. The riots were only the first in what many anticipated to be a wave of Southern assaults on the city. Around Manhattan, whispers spread the news that the worst was yet to come. The headline from that Friday morning's *Times* wondered, "Is the Riot Ended?" Similar questions would recur all through the 1860s and 1870s.[5]

While New Yorkers slowly returned to work on July 17, the city's Catholic leader, Archbishop John Hughes, prepared an address. Notices in the morning's papers had carried a message from Hughes to "the men of New York, who are now called in many of the papers Rioters." The archbishop invited the city's Catholic citizens to hear him speak that afternoon from the balcony of his home at Madison Avenue and 36th Street. Hughes's unfocused remarks failed to make sense of the week's tragedies; in quick succession, Hughes celebrated the Irish community, chastised the rioters, and launched into a series of disconnected political asides. To the gathered Irish Catholic New Yorkers, Hughes stressed, "I cannot see a rioter's face among you."[6] He willed himself, and the crowd, to see what he wished to believe. The archbishop and other Irish leaders would struggle for years to live down their community's role in the riots and to legitimize the Irish presence in the city's public life.

While the archbishop gathered his congregation, many wealthy New Yorkers donated money for the immediate relief of those affected by the riots. Alexander T. Stewart gave five thousand dollars, with the New York Stock Exchange quickly matching the donation. A wave of new organizations formed to distribute the flood of donations and to mobilize citizens in the radically altered postriot political climate. Among these, the Merchants' Committee for the Relief of Colored People Suffering from the Late Riots in the City of New York was especially active in directing aid to the city's embattled African Americans. At the same time, donors and activists often reserved their greatest passion for denouncing the rioters and the city's Irish more generally. As the Republican lawyer George Templeton Strong noted in his diary right after the riots, "I would like to see war made on Irish scum as in 1688." Strong and many other Republicans would, after the riots, assert themselves more directly into municipal politics, attacking what they viewed as the un-American and criminal involvement of the city's Irish.[7]

Opposition to the Conscription Act was by no means limited to New York City. In the summer of 1863 antidraft violence erupted in many other Northern cities, in rural areas of Ohio and Indiana, and in the mining areas of Pennsylvania. The rioters' common slogan—"Rich man's war, poor man's fight"—appealed across the North as the Civil War's third year dragged on. The Manhattan riot's exceptionalism lay in its far greater violence and its sustained length. Further, New York's mayor had suggested the city secede in 1861; by 1863, many of the city's politicians were lined up against Lincoln's war.

New Yorkers struggled to make sense of what they had witnessed on their city's streets for the nearly full week of the rioting. Immediate responses were impassioned, enraged, and disoriented. Quickly, shock gave way to anger and fear. Out of a widespread sense that a conspiracy was at work, several Southerners in the city were arrested.[8] In local newspapers and from the city's pulpits, denunciations of the rioters were linked to the continuing Southern threat. "A Christian Lady," writing to the *Times* a few days after the riots, attacked the city's Irish (especially those Irishwomen who had participated in the violence) while celebrating the humanitarianism of elite Republicans as the only instance of heroism in the otherwise shameful recent history of the city.[9]

Fears of mob violence lingered through the summer of 1863 and shaped the emerging public culture of Gilded Age Manhattan. Those who denounced the mob's actions began to look around the city for other possible threats. One correspondent to the local Republican press voiced particular concern about the mobs of poor "vagrants" who milled around City Hall Park. "Pro Bono Publico" claimed that "they are many of them rebel spies."[10]

By July 24, the Merchants' Committee presented a new institutional face for reform in Manhattan. From offices on East Fourth Street, the committee oversaw the distribution of foodstuffs and other supplies to the city's remaining African Americans, empowering Rev. Henry Highland Garnet to decide who was worthy of assistance. The forty-eight-year-old pastor of Shiloh Presbyterian Church on Prince Street, Garnet was perhaps the city's most eminent, but certainly the most controversial, black minister. A regular antagonist of Frederick Douglass, the preeminent national African American leader of the day, Garnet was also a supporter of some colonization programs. For four decades, many New York African

Americans had struggled against the colonizers' proposed repatriation of free blacks to West Africa. Garnet's work with the African Civilization Society sparked years of debate and controversy among New York's abolitionist community. The Merchants' Committee's choice of Garnet signaled their interest in using the riots to bolster what they considered to be reliably conservative forces in all the city's racial and ethnic communities.[11]

The most important criticism of the draft rioters came not from partisan Republicans but from the Democratic leadership at Tammany Hall. William M. Tweed, emerging as Tammany's leading figure, capitalized on the riots by denouncing any Democratic organization that had been sympathetic to the rioters. Tweed's Tammany Hall established its legitimacy in the immediate aftermath of July's violence. Before the Civil War, the city's Democratic Party had been composed of deeply divided, competing factions. Tweed's particular genius was to see opportunity in the riots. Beginning in July 1863, Tweed presented a public image in opposition to the worst excesses of the rioters, while at the same time attempting to hold off the threat of Republican-directed martial law. Tweed's assistants—District Attorney A. Oakey Hall and City Recorder John T. Hoffman—devoted the rest of the summer to prosecuting rioters, signaling Tammany's commitment to law and order. It would, however, take two years—until Hoffman's election as mayor in 1865—for the Tweed ring to gain full command of the city's democracy.

By the end of the summer, it was difficult to find any public figure with a kind word for the draft riots. George William Curtis, the staunchly Republican editor of *Harper's Weekly*, editorialized that the riots were quickly passing into history, noting how difficult it was to find any "apologists" for "the murderers."[12] Even as he noted such silence, Curtis compared the traitorous behavior of Irish New York with the simultaneous heroism of the African American soldiers in the 54th Massachusetts Regiment, who had fought valiantly at Fort Wagner, South Carolina, in mid-July.[13] It was not lost on Curtis that

> It was at the very hour when negroes were pouring out their blood for the stars and stripes on the slopes of Fort Wagner that naturalized foreigners, who hauled down the Stars and Stripes whenever they saw them, tried to exterminate the negro race in New York.[14]

Curtis's comparison underscored but one way in which the local and the national were linked in the immediate aftermath of July 1863.

In Washington, President Abraham Lincoln sank into a deep melancholy, uncertain as to how to handle the situation in the nation's most important city. Even after Gettysburg, it was by no means clear that the Union army would win the war. Further, the president's hold on New York had always been tenuous. Lincoln's February 1860 visit to the city— during which he delivered his Cooper Union Address and sat for a campaign portrait at Mathew Brady's Broadway studio— had left the westerner feeling just how out of place he was in the metropolis. Once in office, the president was regularly challenged and denounced by the city's large majority of Democratic politicians and voters. Copperheads, or Peace Democrats, in particular, remained opposed to "Lincoln's War" and called for immediate peace. Throughout Lincoln's life, New York City remained inhospitable to him.

Thus, in July 1863, Lincoln's most vigorous supporters in Manhattan urged imposing martial law and the immediate appointment of Gen. Benjamin Butler to command over New

York. Instead, Lincoln sought to ease tensions, appointing Gen. John A. Dix, a War Democrat from Wall Street, the new commander of the Department of the East. From July 1863 on, the president attempted to forge a provisional coalition with conservative New York City Democrats. In hopes of easing Democratic anger, Lincoln resisted his fellow Republicans' calls for a special federal commission to investigate the July violence in Manhattan. Such a commission, the president feared, would "have simply touched a match to a barrel of gunpowder." The presidential solution to the problem was, by and large, to forget the riots as much as possible. In Lincoln's most famous formulation of the issue, "one rebellion at a time is about as much as we can conveniently handle."[15]

Horatio Seymour, the Democratic governor of New York, had long been one of Lincoln's leading critics and a possible opponent in the 1864 presidential campaign. In the early months of 1863, the New Yorker had denounced the proposed conscription; amid the draft riots, he expressed limited support for the rioters. Even after the worst excesses of the rioters had been exposed, Seymour hoped to capitalize on anti-draft sentiment and called for the administration in Washington to eliminate conscription in the Empire State. Rather than reject the proposal out of hand, Lincoln cut the city's draft quota in half, down to twelve thousand. A decided state of stalemate existed between the capitals, state and national.

The municipal government, in turn, earmarked over $2 million to pay for substitutes for Manhattanites; much of this money was directed toward city workers. Other cities around the Empire State quickly followed New York City's lead. As means were found to help white New Yorkers elude the draft, the little criminal prosecution arising from the draft riots sputtered; out of a small number of cases, only a handful of the rioters were ever convicted of crimes. Several Manhattan grand juries refused to hand down indictments, delivering their own verdict on the events of July 1863.

Across the North and the South, the draft riots provoked immediate and intense reaction. The *Richmond Dispatch* gleefully noted "the red battle flag now waves in New York over streets wet with the gore of Lincoln's hated minions."[16] Similar sentiments filled the newspapers of the Confederacy in the summer of 1863; for the rest of the year, the example of a divided New York was held out, by Southerners, as revealing an opponent on the brink of internal collapse.

A radically different interpretation took hold with Northern African Americans. The July violence—and particularly the powerlessness of the city's black men, women, and children—added emphasis to long-standing arguments for an interracial army and equal citizenship. The editors of the *Christian Recorder*, the official organ of the African Methodist Episcopal Church, announced that while the carnage of the riots had ended, the results of the outrage were only beginning to be felt. As it became obvious that white soldiers could not protect the city's black community, the need to empower black soldiers and policemen on the streets of Manhattan grew clear. Once more, the heroism of the Massachusetts 54th was invoked alongside the shame of the draft riots.[17] The strategy of citing the New York riots as reason for black empowerment continued for the remainder of the war.[18]

Reactions to the riots went well beyond the realm of New York politics. The novelist Herman Melville left the Berkshires that summer, returning to Manhattan. The riots deeply affected the author of *Moby-Dick*, inspiring him to write "The House-top. A Night Piece. July, 1863." No other New York writer has so powerfully imagined the horrors of the riots. In countless evocative passages, the poet articulated a rage nearly equal to that found on the city's streets in July, describing "the Atheist roar of riot." The poem's most memorable line portrays "the town . . . taken by it rats—ship-rats and rats of the wharves." Melville's was a pessimistic reading of the riot, the city, and the darkening American mood.[19]

Eight months after the riots, Union Square witnessed the most arresting response to the July 1863 violence. On March 5, 1864, the 20th New York Regiment—an all–African American unit—marched from the Union League headquarters through Manhattan. The *Times* coverage noted that where "eight months ago the African race in this City were literally hunted down like wild beasts," this late winter day found them parading "with waving handkerchiefs, with descending flowers, and with the acclamations and plaudits of countless beholders."[20] For some New Yorkers—black, Republican, abolitionist—this procession was a necessary step in responding to the previous summer's violence.

Yet, even as the men of the Twentieth paraded through the city, and as the Union army moved ever more certainly toward victory, racist criticism was commonplace in the city's public culture. Antiblack anxieties filled the columns of many metropolitan dailies. The *Herald* denounced the possibilities of race-mixing as the "daughters of Fifth Avenue" bestowed colors on the Twentieth. The Workingmen's United Political Association viewed the parade not as signifying an approaching equality of the races, but rather as heralding a new age of black supremacy: "the very object of arming the negroes is based on the instinctive idea of using them to put down the white laboring classes." Such white interpretations of the black freedom struggle in Manhattan would recur throughout the remainder of Reconstruction.[21]

2

BLACK FOUNDERS

At noon on Sunday, February 14, 1865, the Rev. Henry Highland Garnet took to the Speaker's podium in the House of Representatives. An enthusiastic crowd filled the House chamber and spilled out of the galleries into the halls of the Capitol. Black and white, elected official and ordinary citizen, hundreds of Washingtonians came to witness Garnet's address. Garnet made history that day, becoming the first African American ever to deliver a sermon to the House of Representatives. President Lincoln had invited Garnet to commemorate the passage of the Thirteenth Amendment by the Thirty-eighth Congress. Garnet, New York City's leading African American minister for a generation, took the opportunity both to celebrate the abolition of slavery and to attempt an early definition of what was at stake as the war came to an end. In no uncertain terms, Garnet outlined a political, social, and moral program of reconstruction for the nation.[1]

Garnet opened with an extended attack on the institution of slavery, America's "fearful national sin." For a quarter of an hour, he patched together an eclectic argument for abolitionism, invoking among others Plato, Moses, Lafayette, Jonathan Edwards, and Pope Leo X. He reserved his most impassioned rhetoric for a digression on the scribes and Pharisees of biblical times: learned men who were at once legalistic and immoral. Garnet compared modern-day Democrats to these ancient cynics. The minister called special attention to Fernando Wood, his longtime New York foe, former mayor, and congressman. Wood had recently argued in Congress that slavery was "the best possible condition for the negro." For Garnet, such Copperhead beliefs were "unrighteous beyond measure" and demanded censure.[2]

Midway through his sermon, Garnet pressed his attack on Wood and other Northern Democrats by proclaiming that the age of slavery was now dead and the task of defining a new era was at hand. Garnet recognized that many Americans were asking "when and where will the demands of the reformer of this and coming ages end?" Here, Reconstruction—and the possibility of a second founding for the American polity—came front and center as Garnet told the assembled interracial crowd that "great sacrifices have been made by the people; yet, greater still are demanded ere atonement can be made for our national sins." The eloquent minister invoked biblical notions of collective sin and the necessity of atonement to argue for an activist, far-reaching program of Reconstruction. As "the great day of the nation's judgment has come," Garnet challenged his audience to act.

Near the close of his speech, Garnet took on those critics who questioned an activist Reconstruction policy. By February 1865, even before the Civil War ended, some former abolitionists had begun to criticize remedies designed specifically for African Americans. Garnet sought to meet such critics halfway, claiming that "we ask not for special favors, but we plead for justice." Drawing that difference allowed Garnet to finesse the question of government assistance. Stating that blacks should be left to their own devices, he also asked that "in common with others, we may be furnished with rudder, helm and sails, and charts, and compass."

Garnet ended by demanding directly of the assembled congressmen a program of "Emancipation, Enfranchisement, Education . . ." Here, Garnet echoed the numerous national, state, and local conventions of African Americans that had been held in late 1864 and early 1865. Across the nation, the collective voice of African Americans was publicly defining emancipation as but a necessary first step in the larger struggle for racial justice. Suffrage and public schooling filled out Garnet's Northern black program of Reconstruction in early 1865.[3]

African American New Yorkers led the way in defining a radical conception of Reconstruction, both in Manhattan and across the nation. These black framers of the second founding emerged from decades of political struggle in the nation's leading city. Since the early decades of the century, Manhattan had been home to a particularly vibrant network of black churches and community institutions. America's first African American newspaper—*Freedom's Journal*—was launched in the city in 1827. As an important center of free black activism, the city became the capital of the antebellum African American press; fifteen different newspapers and three magazines published out of Manhattan between 1827 and 1865.[4]

Central to the black freedom struggle in New York was the ongoing fight against the legacies of the 1821 state constitutional convention. It was there that a $250 freehold requirement for suffrage, applied only to African American men, had been first codified. Manhattan blacks organized numerous petition drives over the ensuing decades, hoping to persuade the state legislature to amend the constitution so as to grant equal manhood suffrage. The city's black editors and local abolitionists expanded their initial activities of the 1820s and 1830s into a wave of statewide conventions in the 1840s and 1850s, all devoted to the elimination of the property qualification. Thus, for New York's blacks, the coming reconstruction offered an opportunity to nationalize their half-century-old crusade for equal citizenship.

In the fall of 1864, Henry Highland Garnet and five other black Manhattanites traveled upstate to Syracuse to take part in the National Convention of Colored Men. Frederick Douglass, born in slavery in Maryland and by the 1860s the most important African American leader, presided. The assembled black abolitionists debated the meaning of Reconstruction for four days in early October. The simple fact that African Americans were gathering together was a bold statement of political courage; Garnet himself was attacked by an Irish mob on the way to the meeting hall one night. Adding a further and personal insult, George Downing, a longtime leader of New York's black community, roundly criticized Garnet for his work with the African Civilization Society. Having demanded in the 1840s that white abolitionists support slave insurrections in the South, Garnet was by the late 1850s uniting with wealthy whites to form the African Civilization Society, a group devoted to African American emigration. Though Garnet was one of the main organizers of the Syracuse convention and was even nominated to chair the entire meeting, his polarizing image required that other Manhattanites take the podium in Syracuse.[5]

It fell to one of Garnet's closest allies in New York City, Dr. P. B. Randolph, to address the convention on behalf of the city's black community. Randolph, a minister of the A.M.E. Zion Church, seized the opportunity to offer a religious definition of Reconstruction. After numerous biblical allusions, Randolph proclaimed that "the starry flag above our heads . . . is the pledge of heaven, that we are coming up from the long dark night of sorrow towards the morning's dream." Randolph then connected his religious vision of jubilee with a faith in "the great principle of progress." A just Reconstruction would be achieved "not by force of mere appeal, not by loud threats, not by battle-axe and sabre, but by the divine right of brains, of will, of true patriotism, of manhood, of womanhood." Randolph went on to spell out his two primary political demands: the vote and public education. Four months before Garnet took the floor of the House of Representatives, another black Manhattanite was already linking religious deliverance to a practical program of governmental action.

For New York City's black founders, by 1865, any discussion of Reconstruction was primarily a discussion of suffrage. Less than two weeks into the year, Frederick Douglass took the podium at the Cooper Institute to speak to the Ladies' Union Bazaar Association. Douglass's relationship with New York City was always marked by ambivalence, and he never made Manhattan his home base, despite the city's numerous reform organizations and African American publications.

January 1865 marked Douglass's first public appearance in the city since the previous winter. A great orator, he turned his speech into a chance to articulate "the fundamental principle" of Reconstruction: namely, "the absolute and complete enfranchisement of the entire black population of the South." Douglass's pronouncements on the question of Reconstruction were essentially early briefs for the Fifteenth Amendment. And Douglass was not alone in equating Reconstruction with immediate enfranchisement. By the summer of 1865, an African American journalist reported that "the question of universal suffrage is now prominently discussed in the district of Africa, and every colored man wants his voice at the polls."[6]

For the time being, New York's black founders focused their attention on suffrage reform and a general commitment to education. In the winter and early spring of that year, Henry Highland Garnet made several speeches around New York City that echoed his congressional sermon. At an early April meeting at the Cooper Institute in honor of the Thirteenth Amendment, Garnet built on his February address and pushed for integrated schools in New York City and the removal of racial distinctions in the state constitution.[7]

In 1865, however, Garnet was a visitor in, and no longer a resident of, the city. A year earlier, the minister had left his longtime base in Manhattan, the Shiloh Presbyterian Church, for a new post in Washington, D.C. Garnet was drawn to the nation's capital for several reasons. Shiloh had been experiencing financial troubles, a consequence of New York's declining black community, which in the decade after 1855 had dropped from 12,500 to under 10,000. The draft riots of 1863 only hastened black migration from New York City, leaving Shiloh—and all black churches—in dire financial straits.

Driven from New York City by its shrinking black community and wartime racial violence, Garnet was specifically drawn to Washington, D.C., in 1864. That his daughter and her family lived in the capital was a factor, but more important was the politicized public life of the district. In early 1865, Garnet wrote to his long-time friend Martin Delany of his desire "to be close to the center of power." In 1865 and 1866, from the pulpit of Washington's 15th Street Presbyterian Church, Garnet was able to address a national audience. Within the city, he could make more direct appeals to men of influence. He met with various cabinet members and congressmen during his time in D.C.[8]

Garnet's uprootedness was typical of Manhattan's black founders in the early postbellum years. Garnet himself would spend the rest of the decade traveling among Washington, New York, and various points south, advocating congressional Reconstruction, before returning to Manhattan in 1870. At his Washington residence, Garnet hosted in the mid-1860s a broad range of African American political and religious leaders. Like Garnet, they were shuttling between North and South, metropolis and capital, constructing a postbellum black public sphere that provided critical space and support for the black freedom movement. Martin Delany, for one, spent a week at Garnet's Washington home, helping to compose the congressional address of February 14, 1865. A black nationalist who traveled to Africa and received a commission as major in the 104th U.S. Colored Troops, Delany would play a leading role in South Carolina's public life during Reconstruction. Beginning in 1865, numerous African American New Yorkers traveled widely, serving an essential role in the construction and articulation of a black political voice on the national level.[9]

These black founders convinced many Americans to adopt a more radical Republican position on Reconstruction; in turn, they helped put into practice many of the policies of congressional Reconstruction. In their public speeches, through their heroic work in the Deep South, by organizing local and state conventions of freedmen, the black founders of New York forever transformed race relations across America.

Ironically, they did this largely outside of their home city.

Back home in Manhattan, in the two great civic ceremonies of the spring of 1865, black New Yorkers were reminded again of the enduring racism at the heart of public life in the nation's metropolis. The celebration of imminent Union victory in March and Lincoln's funeral procession in April revealed how far New York City was from embracing the ideals of men like Henry Highland Garnet and Frederick Douglass.

To commemorate the Union army's victories in Savannah and Charleston and the rapidly approaching end of the war, a general committee of leading New Yorkers organized a metropolitan celebration of Union victories on March 6. Chaired by Moses Taylor, the conservative Democratic president of the National City Bank of New York, the organizing committee included a broad cross section of New Yorkers, drawn from across party lines and from numerous sectors of the metropolitan economy: Maj. Gen. John A. Dix; prominent Republican lawyer William M. Evarts; even Tammany Hall's William M. Tweed. The parade was originally planned for March 4, but rain postponed the festivities for two days. George Templeton Strong, the Republican attorney and the city's most prolific diarist, was thankful for the delay, since March 4 was also the date of Lincoln's second inaugural in Washington. Strong feared that had the parade been held as originally planned, the city's numerous "anti-Lincolnites" would have stayed home, "lest they should seem to do honor to Lincoln by making the day of his re-inaugural a festival."[10]

As it turned out, Lincolnites and anti-Lincolnites alike turned out in droves two days later as a seven-mile-long procession made its way from Union Square down to Astor Place and on to Canal Street, then back up to 33rd Street before finally returning to Union Square. Over one million spectators watched the parade, a remarkable number in a city of 720,000.

The line of march included three divisions: the military in blue, civic and industrial organizations in black, and two thousand firemen in red. The marchers presented a kaleidoscopic portrait of Manhattan in April 1865: numerous generals, mounted cavalry troops, thousands of metropolitan police, tens of thousands of soldiers-cum-veterans. The city's ethnic communities were represented by, among others, five hundred members of German singing clubs and two hundred members of the Italian Benevolent Association.[11]

Later that day, a jubilant crowd assembled in Union Square to hear a number of speeches; each address shared a strangely unrestrained optimism. The popular Tammany leader A. Oakey Hall saw Reconstruction as a chance for New York to profit from the impending reopening of Southern ports. Another speaker called for New York to resume its rightful place as the nation's leading city. In the next morning's papers, one observer remarked on the "unbroken unity" evident in the parade and ensuing orations.

Few in the mainstream press bothered to point out that this mass display of metropolitan unity was limited to whites only. As the Civil War came to an end, the nation's metropolis staged a fully segregated parade. One of the last speakers at the Union Square rally at last did bring the day's racist undertones to the surface in a discussion of abolitionism, demanding a Reconstruction founded on the principle that the United States "is a government of white men, and should not and shall not be destroyed for the sake of the African." All references to the newly passed Thirteenth Amendment were roundly booed. Strangely, there is little evidence of black protest, but that would change in just over a month.

The assassination of President Lincoln on April 14 presented a new and far more somber opportunity for New York-

ers to reflect on the meanings of the war and prospects for
Reconstruction. On April 25, Lincoln's funeral procession
made its way through Manhattan on its prolonged journey to
Springfield, Illinois. Ten days after the tragic events at Ford's
Theater, the metropolis was still in shock. The fallen president's casket had trekked up from the capital, through Baltimore and Philadelphia; along the way, millions paid their
respects. In Manhattan, one reporter noted the omnipresent
grief: "the city was taking its sad holiday . . . for once church-
going was popular . . . every face has been darkened." George
Templeton Strong was one of the few New Yorkers to find a
slight trace of hope in the events of April 1865. Noting that
"times have changed since July/63!" Strong celebrated "the
depth of popular feeling revealed [by] the demonstration of
public favor shown the societies of black men that joined the
funeral procession."[12]

In planning for the sad event, the New York City Common
Council had initially rejected a petition from local African Americans and decreed that the Manhattan leg of the
thousand-mile funeral procession was to be an all-white affair.
Black New Yorkers quickly mobilized and petitioned the police commissioner, the Union League Club, and others. Finally, at the urging of Garnet and others in Washington,
Charles A. Dana, assistant secretary of war, ordered Maj. Gen.
John A. Dix in New York to use federal troops to enforce
an integrated funeral procession. Over two hundred African
American men marched behind a banner proclaiming "Abraham Lincoln Our Emancipator, To Millions of Bondsmen He
Liberty Gave." Dix's troops and four police platoons marched
alongside, protecting the black contingent from hostile
whites.[13]

The Lincoln funeral procession was an important turning

point for Manhattan's black community. Where Garnet and others had begun the year arguing for a Reconstruction program limited to emancipation and enfranchisement, the realities of unabated metropolitan racism demanded a broader solution. In the months after Lincoln's assassination, black Manhattanites came to articulate a more expansive vision of federal Reconstruction. In particular, local activists began to fight for a nationalized citizenship and a vigorous federal protection of the rights of citizens. At the same time, New York's black founders moved from their local political struggles into more diverse fields. Whether in Washington, D.C., or in the newly freed South, black New Yorkers helped set the terms for the emerging national debates over suffrage, citizenship, and federal power.

Reconstruction was at once a broadly national and an intensely local struggle. For African American New Yorkers, the end of the Civil War in a certain sense marked the end of an era. Manhattan had been a center of the black freedom struggle in America for over a generation, since at least the appearance in 1827 of *Freedom's Journal*, the nation's first black newspaper. In 1865, New York City blacks ever more thoughtfully looked beyond the metropolis to Washington, D.C., and points south. Thereafter, African American debates held throughout the nation during the Reconstruction years often featured New York voices.

As the Civil War concluded, all New Yorkers slowly awakened to the prospect that postbellum America would demand new forms of political action; traditional ways of thinking about public life, it seemed to many, would need to be revised. The antebellum city of memory was gone, and with it the republic of the eighteenth-century founders. In their place, a new New York and a new nation were aborning.

3

TOWARD RECONSTRUCTION

In the late spring of 1865, in the bittersweet weeks after Appomattox and Lincoln's assassination, Walt Whitman set out to collect his poems penned during the Civil War. After sorting through the numerous sketches he had drafted over the previous four years, poems filled with the horrors and the heroism of the battlefield as well as the small mercies of the army hospital, Whitman kept coming back to the need for an epic opening for the collection. For the volume he eventually entitled *Drum-Taps*, the poet chose to write "First O Songs for a Prelude." It depicted his earliest memories of the war: the first months of 1861 in his beloved New York City.

Whitman recalled his "pride and joy in my city, how she led the rest to arms . . ." In just a few short stanzas, Whitman's language rose to typically celebratory heights: "O superb! O Manhattan, my own, my peerless! O strongest you in the hour of danger, in crisis! . . . How you led to the war . . . How Manhattan drum-taps led." The poet imagined the nation's leading city as home to courageous, patriotic New Yorkers, united

in devotion to the just cause of the Union, "young men, me-
chanics, lawyer, judge, driver, salesman, boss, book-keeper,
porter, the blood of the city." From his office at the Bureau of
Indian Affairs in the nation's capital, Whitman's imagination
raced northward into the past.[1]

The romantic vision of Manhattan at the heart of "First O
Songs for a Prelude" was made possible by Whitman's very
distance. From 1861 on, the poet had been back to the city
only for brief visits, and after the war he chose not to return. It
would take a full half decade—until the 1871 publication of
Democratic Vistas—for Whitman to awaken to the more troubling realities of the Civil War and Reconstruction in Manhattan. Those on the ground in New York City during the spring
of 1865 enjoyed none of Whitman's easy nostalgia. Across
Manhattan, New Yorkers struggled to grasp the dimensions of
contemporary social and political upheaval.

In 1865, as the nation prepared to embark on the decade-
long project of Reconstruction, a wide-ranging, intensely contested conversation took place in New York City about its
local meanings. This urban, Northern debate over the second
founding was by no means confined to the city's African
American community but included a disparate collection of
intellectuals, reformers, and politicians. Three institutions—
E. L. Godkin's *Nation*, the Citizens' Association, and the New
York Democratic Party—emerged in 1865 as the leading architects of the first stage of New York's Reconstruction. Each
articulated a particular vision of the second founding for New
Yorkers, while also appealing to national audiences and
constituencies. All three were responding to the idealistic
definition of Reconstruction that had been offered up by
Manhattan's black citizens since July 1863. Extended inquiry
into these three competing visions clarifies the complicated

processes of political and intellectual change in postbellum New York.

On July 6, 1865, the *Nation*'s first issue appeared, promising a new program of reform for the postwar period. Published in New York City, this new weekly set out to cover "Politics, Science, Literature and Art." Most important, the *Nation* afforded its editor, E. L. Godkin, a platform from which to pursue his program of cultural reconstruction, for the city and for America. For the rest of Reconstruction and on to the end of the nineteenth century, Godkin maintained a prominent role in shaping the public life of New York City. The editor's primary contribution in the immediate aftermath of war was to offer up a definition of Reconstruction that stressed education, intelligence, and the development of a cultured elite in America.[2]

Even before the war ended, a new generation of reformers appeared. These young activists published in journals such as the *North American Review* and founded organizations like the American Social Science Association. They sought to fashion for themselves a new public identity: the serious, scientific social critic. At the heart of their project was an emphatic rejection of older, antebellum patterns of social reform that emphasized moral suasion and appeals to sentiment. Godkin's *Nation* perfected this new tone, forging a new form of urban Republicanism while carefully distancing himself from the remains of the antislavery movement. In the first issue, the editor brashly declared

everybody is heartily tired of discussing [the Negro's] condition, and his rights, and yet little else is talked

about, and none talk about him so much as those who
are most convinced of his insignificance.

Godkin was not yet fully prepared to abandon the cause of
the freedpeople; that would take a few years. For the moment, he was satisfied with the resentment he stirred in the
abolitionist community. Godkin proudly reprinted the radical
abolitionist Wendell Phillips's attack on the *Nation*, in which
he decried the magazine's new tone: "How uncertain is its
sound! How timid, vacillating, and noncommittal is its policy." Far from the antebellum Boston of Phillips and William
Lloyd Garrison, Godkin hoped to build in postwar New York
a new type of reform politics.[3]

Godkin was an unlikely figure to emerge as a leading New
York intellectual during Reconstruction. Born in Northern
Ireland, Godkin emigrated to Manhattan as a young man in
the 1850s to work as a journalist. His Civil War stories for the
Daily News helped establish his reputation in the New York
press. At the same time, Godkin developed a lifelong connection with the academic culture of Cambridge, Massachusetts.
His closest correspondent in the 1860s was Charles Eliot Norton, the editor of the *North American Review*, who, with his fellow New England writers, worked with Godkin on the early
editions of the *Nation*. In turn, Godkin's articles for the *North
American Review* earned him an elite national audience even
before the first issue of the *Nation* had appeared.

The cultural reconstruction that Godkin pursued in 1865
and thereafter was premised on the development of an intellectual elite, a national project in which, the editor assumed,
New York City was destined to play the leading role. The
early columns of the *Nation* were filled with concerns over
American culture. One essay, "The Paradise of Mediocrities,"
lamented the ways in which American society hindered

achievement and rewarded mediocrity; it railed against America's "low standard of taste, of morals, and of intellectual performance." The problem, as the editor saw it, was that "there are very few first rate things in America." He proposed the creation of an elite culture of quality, and for the rest of the age of Reconstruction—and for the remainder of his life— Godkin worked to advance the cause of elitism in America.[4]

In his first months as editor, Godkin devoted a number of essays to the question of taste in America. The problem, he diagnosed, lay with the wealthy, especially the "nouveau riche" and their lack of standards. In his columns he returned again and again to the need to resist the corrosive effects of America's evermore market-based culture. Before long, the *Nation* was advocating a return to the ideal of the classical, educated gentleman. Though willing to recognize that times had changed, Godkin argued "there is this much, at least, to be urged in favor of the old standard—that it is a standard." Godkin's early attempts to define Reconstruction—for New York and for the nation—centered on the need to enact standards of taste and intellect.[5]

In 1865 Godkin's *Nation* argued that democratic culture could only be improved through mass education, and that Reconstruction, more than any other era, demanded a recognition of education's importance. "That intelligence lies at the foundation of free institutions," Godkin flatly stated, "is universally recognized." The weekly advocated the creation of a National Board of Education as the centerpiece of federal Reconstruction. Further, Godkin favored the creation of common-school systems as one of the requirements for the readmission of the Southern states. In Manhattan, the editor threw his support behind Councilman White's proposal for funding an elaborate public library system; the library stood as "the natural complement of the public schools . . ." A national system of public libraries, the *Nation* editorialized, would be the best possible investment for the material, moral, and intellectual interests of society.[6]

In the *Nation*, elite New Yorkers questioned the meaning of suffrage and in consequence created a new theory of the right to vote. For Godkin, the new age demanded a new principle: "intelligent suffrage." Racial distinctions were un-American, Godkin explained; instead, "let exclusions be founded on ignorance, not on color." *Nation* editorials mixed a principled vision of racial democracy with unrestrained feelings of class contempt. "Intelligent suffrage" contained within it certain radical possibilities. It could be used—and was used by others—to argue for extensive governmental support for public education for all citizens, including African Americans. Conversely, while rejecting racial exclusion, "intelligent suffrage" opened the way for excluding large numbers of existing voters from the ballot box. In August 1865, Godkin contrasted his admiration for "the freedmen [who] evince in every way an eager desire to be educated" with his abhorrence of "the wilful and persistent ignorance of the poor whites." In discussing universal manhood suffrage publicly and privately, Godkin often repeated a favorite phrase: "the ballot in the hands of an ignorant man may prove but a club in the hands of a blind Samson."[7]

Godkin's ambitious project of cultural reconstruction was at all times tempered by a pronounced pessimism. When he looked around at other reform movements, he warned,

> Reformers in this world have a hard time of it. They are certain while they live to make more enemies than friends, and it is only after they are dead that mankind begins to appreciate them.

Few quotes so neatly capture Godkin's outlook in these years. The editor confined his few hopes to an emerging network of bourgeois clubs. Groups like the Union League Club, the Taxpayers' Union, and the Citizens' Association held out the possibility of an assertive, educated urban elite. The wave of institution building during the 1860s suggested the promise of breaking down the "reticence and taciturnity" of the city's upper class. The new clubs of the postbellum city were a "necessary good," suggesting to Godkin that cultural reconstruction—and progress itself—might just be possible.[8]

While Godkin brought together a circle of reform-minded journalists and professors, other leading New Yorkers set out to articulate other visions of what Reconstruction might mean for the city and the nation.

In December 1863, a few short months after July's draft riots, a group of Manhattan industrialists, merchants, and bankers came together to form the Citizens' Association. At the founding meeting on December 12, members—including Peter Cooper, August Belmont, and Hamilton Fish—dedicated themselves to "effecting a thorough and radical reform in our local government." In its first months of existence, the association declared its primary goals to be "a reduction of our taxes, the protection of our homes and businesses." In the early years of the second founding, the association would broaden its aims and pursue a program of municipal reconstruction, fighting for far-reaching reforms of New York's political world.[9]

One local Citizens' Association supporter voiced the group's definition of Reconstruction in March 1865, proclaiming that the most important work before the nation would involve harmonizing the multitude of too-long-neglected men, women, and children that people our great cities, and swarm in their crowded purlieus. These are the elements of future weal or woe to the republic.

As much as the rural South, urban America—and particularly New York City—required a comprehensive program of reform. The association's leadership was convinced of their work's importance beyond the city's borders. Addressing their "Fellow-Citizens," the association maintained that "if a pure and efficient government can be established in this City, its influence will be felt throughout the whole land." Under the leadership of the banker James Brown in 1865 and Peter Cooper thereafter, the group's membership pursued an aggressive local and national campaign to clean up public life. The association organized public meetings, published pamphlets, sent delegates to lobby in Albany, and proposed elaborate and dramatic reforms for municipal government. Over two million copies of the association's publications were distributed in 1865; before 1866 was out the group had convened over three hundred public meetings.[10]

The Citizens' Association's most significant early entry into the city's public life came with the publication of its *Report on Sanitary Conditions* in Manhattan. The document was the first shot in the postbellum reform campaigns waged by the city's middle class during the Reconstruction years. This initial articulation of a new reform ideology was largely written by the association's numerous medical members, in language clinical by nature. Taking its lead from the wartime service of the U.S. Sanitary Commission, New York's Citizens' Association expanded from a concern with public health to a much more ambitious urban reform agenda.[11]

Throughout 1865, the association's members embarked on a wide-ranging publicity campaign, speaking all over Manhattan, writing articles for sympathetic dailies and weeklies. Nearly all pronouncements began with a similar mantra, taken from the sanitary report: "New York to-day is the filthiest and the most unhealthy city to be found within the limits of the civilized world." The individual record books of the association's fifteen sanitary inspectors highlight the mixture of medical concern and class anxiety that fueled the group's obsessions. Despite individual differences, all of the association's inspectors shared certain interests. Appropriately for a group founded in the aftermath of the draft riots, all inspectors documented the African American community in some detail. The city's shrinking black population was noted in ward after ward. On Sullivan Street, a neighborhood "occupied by negroes previous to the riot" was now a German district. All over Manhattan, association members found that "the colored population formerly so numerous have almost entirely disappeared." The various inspectors, furthermore, all linked descriptions of a neighborhood's public health conditions to an appraisal of the moral character of the community, with healthy areas populated by the "respectable" while the "disreputable" gravitated toward diseased quarters. Dr. Oscar Smith, a particularly precise recorder of local conditions, provided his own personal map of the moral and medical conditions of the East Side.[12]

Association members quickly expanded such alarmist language beyond the merely medical and sounded a call for rapid and total change in the city's institutional structure. This public health hysteria escalated in the late summer of 1865, as rumors of an impending cholera outbreak swept through the city. The Citizens' Association sprang into action, helping to create the Metropolitan Board of Health a year later. One association supporter was even enthusiastic over the prospect of a cholera epidemic:

> [T]he cholera is likely to be to us what M. Hausmann is to Paris. In view of its approach, those quarters of our great cities which have been heedlessly tolerated until now, will be erased from the map.[13]

The prime target of municipal reconstruction was New York's city government and its elected officials. No language was too extreme for the association's attacks on the local administration. As defined by the association, municipal reconstruction came to have two primary goals: franchise reform and fiscal retrenchment. As the question of black suffrage moved toward the center of national debate, the association launched a crusade to restore the "purity of the ballot box" in Manhattan. During the second founding, the association's elite membership substantially lost faith in mass suffrage. The votes of workingmen were seen as "subduing" the city's taxpayers, and many members came to look favorably upon proposals to restrict suffrage along class lines.[14]

Linked to this intensifying distrust of mass suffrage was a blistering attack on the size and scope of municipal government. A series of association pamphlets exposed corruption in nearly every city agency: among the targets were schools, street cleaners, and public markets. The group lobbied for the passage of a new tax levy bill that would have prohibited the Common Council from creating any new office or department. To justify their reform campaigns and regular calls for new legislation, the Citizens' Association claimed to have "already saved our citizens millions of dollars." Municipal reconstruction, the association claimed, was a matter of simple common sense.[15]

Even as the Citizens' Association members imagined they were fighting for the public's interests, many other New Yorkers questioned the reformers' program of electoral and municipal reform. The association's political work revealed the widening class divisions that would characterize the postwar metropolis. As early as January 1865, three months before Appomattox, the first eruption of class conflict over municipal reconstruction occurred. Two weeks into the new year, the municipal street cleaners struck in demand of their full wages for work already completed. This work stoppage—and the accompanying debate—marked the beginning of anti–Citizens' Association agitation in Manhattan.

The association had achieved a minor political success the previous fall, electing John Hecker as alderman. Hecker viewed the graft-laden street cleaning contract—an issue that simultaneously touched on the city's sanitary and financial health—as a ripe target for reform. In January 1865, the new alderman succeeded in stopping payment to the street cleaners, precipitating a revolt among the city's municipal workers. The labor and ethnic press was particularly outraged; one paper editorialized "if the Citizens' Association can give no better earnest of their ability as reformers, the sooner they disband the better it will be for themselves and the City."

Class lines were quickly and starkly drawn. The *Irish American* sarcastically suggested that

> Mr. Hecker and his associates are generally men well to do in this world; and it may be good that while leisurely digesting a good Christmas dinner of roast beef, turkey, and plum pudding, they may wonder how a laborer, to

whom the city owes a month's wages, for work done, can be hungry or cold, or wanting this money that he has honestly earned, his wife and little ones must go supperless to bed . . .

Manhattan's street cleaners advanced their claims on the city's government by appropriating the identity of citizen. At a January 15 mass meeting of municipal workers in City Hall Park, one speaker demanded full payment to the street cleaners and continued employment "in recognition of our rights as citizens and our just dues as working men." At the dawn of Reconstruction, the metropolitan labor movement began to demand large-scale governmental employment in terms of fundamental citizens' rights.[16]

This bold new conception of "the rights of citizens" deeply troubled the members of the Citizens' Association and other elite New Yorkers. For the next decade, leading Manhattanites would campaign to delegitimize such claims, depicting public works and government employment as inherently corrupt and inefficient. Central to the reformers' rhetoric throughout these years was their identity as taxpayers. Against the idea of workers' rights would be invoked the theory of taxpayers' special rights. In early 1865, however, the Citizens' Association had yet to perfect such a strategy. After the street cleaners were victorious and John Hecker was forced to back down, the pro–Citizens' Association *Tribune* could only warn that

we must wait until the income of our real estate is entirely swallowed up by taxation, and then perhaps the Tax-payers will do something. Now, the great mass of them are sleeping.[17]

The Citizens' Association's membership, in common with the readership of Godkin's *Nation*, imagined metropolitan reconstruction as a reformer's delight. Elite stewardship, clean government, nonpartisan administration—many Manhattan reformers shared these goals as the Civil War ended. Standing in the way of such reform dreams, however, lay the entrenched political powers of the New York City Democratic Party. And the Democrats too offered up their own vision of a reconstructed New York.

The city's Democratic Party found itself in a strange position in 1865. It could still rely on the fact that for several decades the city had been one of the party's centers of strength. Since the age of Jackson, national Democrats had relied on the Manhattan organization for votes and money. However, the party's legitimacy both locally and nationally was now vulnerable due to its wartime record of, at best, lukewarm support for the Union cause. Many local Democrats had been boisterous in their opposition to the Lincoln administration and extreme in their statements of sympathy for the Confederate cause. The Mozart Hall wing of the party—led by the one-time mayor and congressman Fernando Wood—had been conspicuous in its leadership of the Peace Democracy movement throughout the war.[18]

That association abetted the war's most immediate result: the consolidation of Tammany Hall's position as the dominant faction within the Democratic Party. Tammany's ascension was founded on the two central planks in its platform: ritualized professions of nationalism and vigorous support for public works. The highlight of Tammany's year was its annual July Fourth celebration, when the sachems and the rank-and-file came together to point to Mozart Hall's treasonous past and proclaim their own devotion to the Union cause, however narrowly conceived. Such public displays of Tammany-style patriotism enabled many Democrats to overcome the accusation of having been wartime Copperheads. A vast program of public construction and governmental employment was the second critical component of the postbellum Democratic Party. Massive expenditures on street construction were the key to gaining the support of a broad coalition of builders, immigrant workers, and real estate speculators.[19]

But it was Tammany's racialized vision of a white man's reconstruction that proved most explosive in 1865 and would have the greatest impact on the second founding in Manhattan and across America. New York's Democratic politicians were unabashed in their rejection of all definitions of Reconstruction that would lead to interracial democracy. Two Manhattan congressmen voted against the Thirteenth Amendment's abolition of slavery in 1865 and Democratic publicists and editors, like John van Evrie of the *Weekly Day Book*, were the principal architects of the white supremacist wave of the late sixties that appealed to antiblack audiences across postwar America. The metropolitan party apparatus presented a united front in opposition to the radical Republican program.

New York's Democracy came together in late 1866 to announce its adamant opposition to federal Reconstruction, an opposition largely founded upon racial ideology. In support of Andrew Johnson, the embattled president already marked for impeachment by some Republicans, Manhattan Democrats organized a "monster mass meeting" to be held in Union Square on September 17, 1866, the anniversary of the 1787 adoption of the Constitution in Philadelphia.[20]

Over a hundred thousand Manhattanites filled Union Square and the surrounding streets on the night of the seventeenth. An imposing grandstand towered over the Broadway gate to the square, beaming luminous transparencies and flooding the assembled crowd with calcium light. At the center of the stand, a giant portrait of President Johnson was framed by the inscription, "so far as in me lies, I intend to administer the government upon the principles that lie at the foundation of it." Giant banners hung at three corners of the square, proclaiming "One Country, One Constitution, One Destiny"; "The Constitution is My League"; and "Eternal Hostility to every Form of Tyranny."

Maj. Gen. John A. Dix, the conservative Democrat Lincoln had placed in command of New York in the days after the 1863 draft riots, chaired the proceedings. His well-received speech cataloged the alleged injustices then being inflicted on white Southerners. Dix's address reached its most impassioned moment when he discussed New York City's relation to Reconstruction; he rhetorically asked,

> is any man so biased as not to see that this injustice is reacting on us, on our growth, our production, our wealth, our whole social capacity for useful and successful progress?

For the general, and for many Democratic New Yorkers, the current radical Republican policy posed an economic threat to the city. Dix's assertion that federal Reconstruction in the South "is encumbering us with pecuniary burdens," was an early articulation of the fiscal conservative challenge to federal policy in the South that would intensify in the coming decade.

The evening's most important moment came when Samuel J. Tilden, a leading corporate lawyer, took the podium. This pro-Johnson rally signaled Tilden's new position as a leading voice of the New York State Democracy, a position he would keep for the remainder of Reconstruction. His speech that night illuminated the various strands—economic, constitutional, racist—of the Democratic Party's project of white man's reconstruction. Tilden opened his remarks by attacking Radical Republicans in Congress and proceeded to demand a return to America's alleged states' rights traditions. Less than eighteen months after the Civil War's end, it was already possible to argue for a reconstructed nation founded on the principles of state sovereignty evoked at the nation's inception and so deeply contested over the first six and a half decades of the nineteenth century.[21]

Active in metropolitan Democratic politics since the 1830s, when he arrived in Manhattan as a young lawyer from upstate, Tilden had been surprisingly vocal in support of Copperhead causes during the Civil War. Only in the fall of 1866 did he consolidate his position as the chairman of the state Democratic Party. Tilden was the rarity, able to negotiate among the competing claims of E. L. Godkin, the Citizens' Association, and the Democratic Party. He was also especially skillful at appealing to a wide range of audiences in Manhattan and across the country. The one constituency with whom Tilden—the master negotiator—never sought to find common ground was the city's African American community. In pursuit of his dream of a postwar America under Democratic rule, Tilden crafted an ideology of white man's reconstruction.[22]

Tilden's Union Square address primarily dwelt upon the U.S. Constitution, which he declared "to be perpetual." This was essential for Tilden's argument because he went on to assert that it was therefore impossible for any state to have ever seceded; thus the Southern states were "all now in the

Union." This meant that federal Reconstruction—which was dividing the South into five separate military districts—was not only unnecessary but unconstitutional. Additionally, Tilden suggested that white Southerners could immediately vote in that fall's elections, a powerfully appealing prospect for a Northern Democrat.

This constitutional theory led Tilden to believe that any further federal Reconstruction could prove both "costly" and "fruitless." With the war over, he demanded that the overriding goal of all policy be the reestablishment of the nation's "great traditions of constitutional government, founded on local self-control." This emphasis on "local self-control" lay at the heart of Tilden's definition of Reconstruction as restoration. The "centralism" of the congressional Republicans endangered America's most cherished political traditions, Tilden warned, threatening the "erection upon this fair continent [of] eleven Polands—eleven Hungaries—eleven Irelands!" In 1866, Tilden returned to this threatened despotism in nearly all of his public statements. Concern for white Southern autonomy easily merged into fear for self-rule in New York; as he had told a party assembly that summer, "the same principles which they would apply to our recent enemies, they freely extend to the whole Northern people."[23]

Tilden's formulation became the dominant rhetorical mode for Northern Democrats in the 1866 congressional campaign. As he campaigned across the North with former New York governor and prospective 1868 presidential candidate Horatio Seymour, the two men repeatedly linked Southern issues to local New York concerns in their pursuit of a national white man's Reconstruction. At each campaign stop, the speeches of Tilden, Seymour, and other party leaders were followed by the singing of "We Are Coming," the Democrats' preferred campaign song. The chorus made clear the New York Democracy's attack on Republicans and on Reconstruction more generally:

> We are coming with justice to upbraid your party for its blundering and the bad laws it has made; It has sunk the country deep in debt, to carry out its spite—To elevate the black man . . . and trample on the white.

As thousands of Democrats paraded through Manhattan after one late October mass meeting, numerous Democratic clubs marched behind the same banner: "The Negro May Become a Republican, a Slave, or a Tyrant!; but Never a Democrat." For New York City Democrats, affairs of party were now strictly affairs of race.[24]

PART TWO

A NEW POLITICS

(1866–1874)

4

AN AGE OF CONVENTIONS

On the morning of December 6, 1865, Congressman John A. Bingham, a Republican from Ohio, introduced the single most significant piece of the congressional Republican platform for Reconstruction: the Fourteenth Amendment. Earlier in the year, with the passage of the Thirteenth Amendment, this process had been employed to abolish slavery forever in the United States.[1] As the new Thirty-ninth Congress convened, Bingham proposed to

> amend the Constitution of the United States so as to empower Congress to pass all necessary and proper laws to secure to all persons in every State of the Union equal protection in their rights, life, liberty, and property . . .

The question of the hour was: should full citizenship and with it "equal protection" be extended to African Americans, North and South? Equality—legal, political, and social —emerged as the dominant political issue of the coming legislative session. Indeed, the twelve-year drama of Reconstruction was in large part a sustained struggle over the dimensions and consequences of Bingham's proposed amendment. As 1865 drew to a close, with New Yorkers engaged in an intensifying and explosive debate over the programs and purposes of Reconstruction—both local and national—Republicans in Washington, D.C., pressed the question of equal citizenship and interracial democracy.[2]

Within a week of Bingham's presenting his proposed amendment, New York City emerged as the center of opposition. John Chanler, one of the most notoriously racist members of Manhattan's congressional delegation, led his fellow New York Democrats, and many other Northerners, in vigorous and sustained resistance to the Fourteenth Amendment and full black citizenship. Taking the floor of the House of Representatives on December 13, 1865, Chanler affirmed the New York Democratic Party's resistance to ascendant Radical Republicanism. The combative New Yorker opened by countering recent Republican celebrations of the past year's accomplishments. Chanler objected even to moderates who might "consider that the problem of the negro race is solved." Rather, the Democrat took exception to any of his Republican colleagues who proposed "the black man is our equal." Such egalitarian notions, Chanler announced, were "an insult to the white citizens of the United States." Chanler was one of Manhattan's many public figures who rushed to attack the proposed Fourteenth Amendment in the last weeks of 1865 and the first months of 1866. The Civil War had done little to convert New Yorkers like John Chanler from long-held beliefs in white supremacy.

Chanler's opposition to the amendment, founded upon his belief in the natural inequality of the races, brought together competing ideas about African American power and powerlessness. Addressing Bingham and other congressional Republicans, Chanler warned, "You are endeavoring to raise the negro to an equality with the white race for which he is not fit." Quickly, Chanler turned his attack on the proposed amendment into a disingenuous defense of the interests of black Americans. This New York Copperhead, who had helped stoke the flames of white racism throughout Manhattan in the months before the draft riots, now presumed to counsel the Radicals on how best to protect freedmen and -women: "you are unwise in seeking to place him in a position, the duties of which he cannot comprehend, and to expose him to dangers with which he is not competent to cope." Chanler concluded by injecting one final bit of unreconstructed racism, announcing that he and his fellow New York Democrats "have had enough of this love and zeal for the black race. It is an epidemic akin to the black vomit."[3]

In this first speech by a New Yorker in opposition to the Fourteenth Amendment, elements of antebellum Democratic rhetoric commingle with some of the worst appeals to white self-interest. Less than thirty months from the riots of July 1863, African American New Yorkers who read Chanler's remarks—they were republished throughout the metropolitan press over the next few days—could have detected the ratcheting up in scale and intensity of political white supremacy. Chanler's arguments swung from traditional partisan appeals to insincere proclamations of Democratic paternalism. Most arresting was the congressman's call for an end to the "epidemic" of problack feeling. The year 1865 had not yet ended and already leading New York City Democrats were labeling all Reconstruction legislation excessive and no longer necessary.

It took barely another month for John Chanler to perfect a New York language of opposition to the Fourteenth Amendment and congressional Reconstruction. Taking the House floor on January 12, 1866, the Manhattan Democrat pronounced without hesitation, "this is a white workingman's government." Chanler's rambling interpretation of the recently concluded "white man's civil war" blended obscure constitutional precedent, nationalistic popular history, and pseudoscientific racial theorizing. In this early 1866 speech, whiteness became the defining characteristic of American citizenship. Further disputing Radical claims of racial equality, Chanler rejected the very possibility of black participation in self-rule, arguing that while "white democracy makes war on every class, caste, and race which assails its sovereignty . . . Black democracy does not exist." With impassioned rhetoric, the Democratic firebrand warned his fellow congressmen that "by establishing equality, social and public," America was "inducing" a race war. His message was unequivocal: not only were the races unequal; their interests were in direct and potentially violent opposition to each other.[4]

John Chanler confined his definition of equality to the "white man's democracy," an antebellum idea with strong appeal after the Civil War. In New York City during the age of Reconstruction, Chanler was by no means an isolated voice. From late 1865 on, the metropolis was the Northern capital of anti-Reconstruction activism. The Fourteenth and Fifteenth Amendments would in time be opposed by many white Manhattanites. Historian David Montgomery is certainly correct to argue for class conflict as "the submerged shoal on which Radical dreams foundered." More important, however, at least in the nation's largest city, Northern white racism—and especially politically driven racism—was the very visible roadblock into which radical dreams crashed.

———

In 1866, as Congressman Chanler and the New York Democratic Party pursued its program of white man's Reconstruction, African Americans in New York came together that October in Albany for a Convention of Colored Men. Manhattan's black community sent six delegates. The assembled African Americans, well aware of the racist backlash that was sweeping the North, agreed that the most important work before them was to plan for "the approaching Constitutional Convention" in New York State. The body resolved to demand that a constitutional convention be held in 1867 and that the long-despised suffrage restriction on black men be removed as soon as possible from the state's constitution.[5]

As early as January 1865, Rev. Henry Bellows, the white Manhattanite who had led the U.S. Sanitary Commission during the war, had been leading the city's Union League Club in calling for a constitutional convention. As the Civil War raged on, Bellows demanded the chance to remedy "the political evils under which we suffer." A year later, most New York Republicans had joined the Union League Club in seeking a convention. It was assumed the state's postbellum Republican majority, under Gov. Reuben Fenton's leadership, would manage to rewrite the state constitution in keeping with the principles of Lincoln. Many Republicans anticipated that a convention would be the party's crowning achievement during its first decade in power. Of course, New York Democrats first organized against convening a convention and then in opposition to the Republican platform at the convention of 1867–1868. New York's convention was part of a larger national effort to remake state constitutions in the immediate postwar years, as several other Northern states joined their Southern counterparts in holding revision conventions.[6]

Manhattan's African American organizations had long argued for a thorough revision of the state constitution. In the state elections of 1846 and 1860, however, the Empire State's voters opted to maintain the racially discriminatory property qualification. By 1867, New York blacks would be among the first to lobby the new convention for action on the issue of suffrage. The Colored Citizens State Central Committee, led by Dr. William H. Johnson, invoked the Declaration of Independence in defining the great issue of the coming convention as "impartial manhood suffrage."[7]

The 1866 reelection of Governor Fenton prepared the way for the first state constitutional convention in a generation. In his annual message in early 1867, Fenton reminded his Democratic critics that a November 1866 statewide referendum had overwhelmingly approved the call for a revision convention. The governor stated that the referendum's passage revealed "an emphatic expression of the public judgment that some modification of the organic law is essential to the general welfare." It would take the remainder of the decade for New Yorkers to agree as to just what modifications of the organic law were essential. Much of the 1867 legislative session in both the assembly and the state senate was devoted to establishing the proper ground rules for the upcoming constitutional convention. The two parties debated extensively the most basic technical questions. The site of the convention was the subject of great controversy, as was its timing. The state legislature took weeks to agree on apportionment and the proper means of electing delegates. Democrats sought to hold the convention in Manhattan. Republicans proposed that black men should vote for delegates according to the same suffrage requirements as white men.[8]

Governor Fenton's Republican allies gained the upper hand on nearly all procedural issues. The convention, it was decided, would be held in Albany, far removed from New

York City's combative Democratic masses. In fact, on only one central issue were Republicans forced to retreat; existing property qualifications would apply in the selection of convention delegates. "Impartial manhood suffrage" would have to wait, as by a vote of ninety to thirty-three the Republican-controlled assembly decided to maintain existing qualifications for the special election on April 20. Among the eminent New Yorkers elected to take part in the constitutional convention as delegates were Samuel J. Tilden, the Democrats' state chairman, and Horace Greeley, the Republican editor of the *Tribune*.[9]

Delegates convened in Albany on June 4, quickly selecting as president William A. Wheeler, the upstate Republican who had served in the state legislature, in Congress, and as president of the New York Northern Railroad. Upon his election, Wheeler offered a sweeping vision of the convention's purpose:

> we owe it to the cause of universal civil liberty, we owe it to the struggling liberalism of the old world, . . . that every man within [New York], of whatever race or color, or however poor, helpless or lowly he may be, in virtue of his manhood, is entitled to the full employment of every right appertaining to the most exalted citizenship.

Even as he prepared to appoint twenty-seven different committees on subjects ranging from canals to taxation, Wheeler made it clear that the achievement of an interracial democracy was the convention's primary objective.[10]

Delegates offered a wide range of proposals to the various committees in the convention's first weeks. It must have seemed as though every Empire State reformer had descended upon Albany. On June 11, one delegate called for a referendum on women's suffrage on which only women could vote. Three days later, he demanded immediate prohibition of the sale of alcohol in New York. Another delegate demanded that the preamble be amended to include repeated references to "Almighty God." Soon came a request for proportional representation. Calls for compulsory education were immediately followed by demands for Indian rights. The state law for capital punishment was challenged.[11]

The freewheeling early course of the convention quickly gave way to a sustained focus on a handful of defining issues, most especially African American manhood suffrage. Since 1821, black men—and only black men—had been subject to a property-holding requirement in order to vote in New York; no such property qualification applied to the state's white men. The Committee on the Right of Suffrage turned out to be the lightning rod of controversy throughout the convention's many months of deliberations. Headed by Horace Greeley and including no Manhattan Democrats, the Greeley Committee (as it was immediately and permanently identified) was inundated with hundreds of petitions in the summer of 1867; New Yorkers came forth in large numbers to demand, among other proposals, women's suffrage, a reduction of the voting age to eighteen, and a reimposition of property qualifications for the state's white men. Greeley was one of only two downstate members of his committee; the other was John G. Schumaker of Brooklyn. The committee's leading Democrat was William Cassidy, editor of the Albany *Argus*.[12]

It was left to this seven-member committee to decide whether, in the wake of the Civil War and emancipation, New York would remove the property qualification for black voters.

The 1821 state constitution had removed property qualifications on suffrage for New York's poor white men. That same convention—and its successor in 1846—had singled out African American men for a special, exclusionary requirement; to vote, blacks had to own at least $250 in property on which they paid taxes. For nearly half a century, the vast majority of the Empire State's African American men had been effectively disfranchised. From the moment the Greeley Committee first met in the summer of 1867 until the decade came to a close thirty months later, the debate over whether or not to remove the 1821 property qualification came to define the very meaning of Reconstruction in New York.[13]

Horace Greeley, for over a quarter century a leading voice of metropolitan and national reform, had made it clear even before the end of the Civil War that he was an advocate of equal manhood suffrage, or, as he defined it, "impartial suffrage." In the first postwar years, the editor was often decidedly optimistic about the coming struggles for reform, both in New York City and across the nation. As the convention approached and Greeley grew convinced of the overriding necessity of achieving equal manhood suffrage, pessimism crept into his private correspondence. In late 1866, he warned his fellow Republicans that "if we shall close this long controversy with the negro still a serf, we shall be a beaten bankrupt party."[14]

Under Greeley's leadership, the committee's Republican majority quickly proposed the removal of the property qualification for African Americans. By June 28, less than a month into the convention, the Greeley Committee submitted a new article on suffrage for the state constitution with no mention of race. According to the proposed article, all men over twenty-one years of age who had been in New York for one year, who resided in an election district for one month, and who had been citizens for thirty days could vote. The naturalization requirement for new citizens would be increased from ten to thirty days. The committee proposed two critical qualifications: "adult rational manhood" and "exemption from dependence on others." "Idiots, lunatics, . . . felons," among others, were thus to be excluded. One special provision—inspired by the experience of the Civil War—changed the law to guarantee no loss of residency due to military service. Greeley reserved his strongest language for attacking the existing property qualifications: "we can imagine no tolerable excuse for perpetuating the existing proscription." The Committee on Suffrage argued that true equality required the elimination of legal discriminations based on race.[15]

Before closing its report, the Greeley Committee commented on several proposals it had rejected. While a voting age of eighteen and a poll tax were immediately dismissed, the members devoted a good deal more time to the possibilities of a literacy test and of women's suffrage. While attracted to the idea of the former, the committee decided that, given the fact that the illiterate served in the nation's military, such a requirement would be unjust. In the aftermath of the Civil War, linking military service to citizenship was common. As to women's suffrage, in spite of what the committee recognized as solid arguments in favor, the members sensed that the public was not prepared for such a reform. In essence, the Greeley Committee hoped that black suffrage would be viewed as less "revolutionary and sweeping" than women's suffrage.[16]

Troubling signs immediately appeared. Less than two weeks after his committee had issued its report, Greeley wrote to a friend: "I am in the midst of a debate on my own Report on Suffrage, with the current running strongly against me . . ."[17]

Greeley's egalitarian hopes were undercut immediately on June 28, when the Democrats on his committee issued a minority report. Written by William Cassidy, the report demanded that, as in 1846 and 1860, the property qualifications be put to a separate referendum, one removed from the revised constitution. In preparing his report, Cassidy was in regular contact with Democratic state chairman, Samuel J. Tilden, and the final version contains various echoes of Tilden's longtime opposition to equal manhood suffrage. The minority report advanced various arguments and suggested a range of possible reforms, but focused primarily on the issue of separate submission. By the end of the year, that issue would come to undermine the entire convention. In the summer of 1867, however, the Greeley Committee's majority report was adopted by the committee of the whole on July 30, with only the naturalization revision dropped.[18]

While delegates in Albany began what would be a yearlong debate on black suffrage, New York City reformers sought to move from the question of racial voting to the problem of urban voting. The Citizens' Association, in a series of pamphlets issued in 1867, attempted to pressure the convention's delegates to take action on suffrage in the state's largest city. Peter Cooper, the association's chair, authored the first such pamphlet; in it, he called for strengthened powers for unelected commissions. Succeeding pamphlets attacked the problem of suffrage restriction from a number of angles. The association suggested a prohibitive five-thousand-dollar property qualification for a proposed Board of Councilmen. The goal was to place complete control of the city's finances in the hands of Manhattan's richest taxpayers. The association went so far as to propose an office-holding property requirement for councilmen of thirty thousand dollars. The Citizens' Association also floated a plan for a system of local taxpayer juries in

New York City. Taxpayers who owned over twenty thousand dollars in property would serve by lot. Each year these elite panels would have the power to authorize or reject all municipal taxes. One last proposal carried the association's reform schemes to their logical conclusion: suburbanites who paid taxes in New York City would have the right to vote in municipal elections. The ownership of property and the payment of taxes on that property would serve as the basis for political participation in the nation's leading city. For the first time in New York during the second founding, political equality was challenged by a still-forming ideology of taxpayers' special rights.[19]

George Opdyke, former Republican mayor of New York City, took up the Citizens' Association campaign in his position on the Convention's Committee on Cities. In many ways a full decade ahead of his time, Opdyke led a small dissenting minority on the committee and distanced himself from his party's Radical delegates, rejecting any talk of suffrage for "all men" as "too broad." Universal suffrage, for Opdyke, was at odds with the public good; therefore, he proposed that suffrage in New York's cities be limited to taxpayers who owned at least one thousand dollars in property. In Opdyke's view, any broader basis for the right of suffrage was "suicidal." It would take nearly a decade for such ideas to gain wider currency.[20]

Not every municipal reformer in 1867 was prepared to limit the vote along class lines. Alternative systems of suffrage reform appeared all over New York. Speaking for the Personal Representation Society before the Committee on Cities, the young lawyer Simon Sterne offered a rather unusual plan to the convention. Wary of the growing powers of uneducated urban voters, Sterne recommended the ideas of the British theorist Thomas Hare, the leading advocate of cumulative voting in the mid-nineteenth century. The Personal Representation Society advocated just such a system for New York City, employing a language of political equality to argue for the need to balance the votes of the majority with the "refinement and civilization" of the educated classes. In the midst of the Republican-controlled convention in Albany, various reform associations and societies initiated a decade-long assault on popular government in Manhattan. Several of these plans and their architects would take central roles in the very different political culture of the 1870s.[21]

New York City Democrats enthusiastically took up the battle against black suffrage in particular and the convention in general. Tammany publicists accused the delegates of creating a new "upper house" of the state government. Thwarting the prospect of race-blind manhood suffrage moved to the center of Democratic politics for the remainder of the 1860s in New York. Visions of intermarriage and "Negro supremacy" were preferred means of attack. The *Freeman's Journal*, a leading local Irish Catholic weekly that had long denounced abolitionism, recommended that the property qualification be discarded and all African Americans be disfranchised.[22]

As summer turned into fall and early Republican hopes gave way to greater Democratic obstructionism, it was apparent that the local fall campaign would determine just how much of the majority's program would be enacted. Horace Greeley's deepening pessimism was typical of Republican delegates. In August, after just two months in Albany, the editor wrote, "I am working very hard here, and am very sorry I ever came to the Convention." Greeley's regret intensified as he watched Democratic delegates grow ever more assertive. The Democratic call for "separate submission—a November ballot with two referenda, one on suffrage reform, the other the amended constitution—was advanced in the language of self-rule and states' rights and quickly proved effective. Greeley and other Republicans were unable to combat Democratic success at defining black exclusion as a "matter of democracy." Before long, even the reform-minded New York *Citizen* embraced the logic of separate referenda.[23]

In the face of mounting pressure for separate submission and growing dissension from his Republican majority, William A. Wheeler adjourned the convention from September 12 until November 12: the entire fall campaign season. When news of Wheeler's decision reached Manhattan, the city's Democratic leadership rejoiced; Tammany's campaign broadside, *The Alarm Bell of Liberty*, asked, "Is this negro EQUALITY, or is it intended to promote NEGRO SUPREMACY in the Empire State?" The question, of course, was rhetorical. Democrats seized upon an issue and a slogan that would prove successful for the rest of the decade: black political equality would mean black political dominance. State and city elections in 1867, 1868, and 1869 would all be won by Democratic candidates on the strength of this interpretation of black citizenship.[24]

On October 16, midway between the convention's adjournment and election day, Mayor John Hoffman chaired a meeting of Manhattan Democrats at the Masonic Hall on Thirteenth Street. The mayor pointed to the upcoming contest as an opportunity for "moderate conservative men" to challenge Radical rule in Washington and in Albany. Hoffman denounced the very idea of black equality, promising

> The people of the North are not willing . . . that there should be negro judges, negro magistrates, negro jurors, negro legislators, negro Congressmen.

The popular Tammany mayor—and future governor—raged at length at black enfranchisement, reserving his final anger for the members of the Union League Club and their program of "universal negro suffrage and proscriptive white suffrage." Hoffman was followed to the platform that evening by Samuel J. Tilden, home from his responsibilities as a delegate in Albany. Tilden added one last reason for Manhattanites to vote Democratic in November. Tilden claimed that with African American suffrage "it is not merely the white race of the South that is to be borne down . . . It is ourselves also . . . It is, therefore, for our own emancipation that we strike today." The freedom of white New Yorkers, Tilden argued, depended on the continued disfranchisement of the state's African Americans.[25] The Republican Party suffered a crushing defeat in the state elections of 1867. In New York City, the Democrats achieved a majority of over sixty thousand. Before a large crowd celebrating on election night at Tammany Hall, Capt. Isaiah Rynders proposed three hearty cheers for "the white man's party" and went on to define the meaning of the Democratic victory. Thousands cheered Rynders's assertion that "the white race were again in the ascendant."[26]

Up the river in Albany, delegates reconvened on November 12, but by early December the convention again adjourned, this time until after the new year. When the convention regathered in January 1868, the delegates and their work had become the subject of withering ridicule from across the state. The New York *Citizen* spoke of the convention as a "poor motherless, fatherless waif," which was apt to be "cut off in the prime of its youth." As public interest in the convention waned, "the hotel keepers of Albany [were] the only ones who . . . desire its continuance." With public support rapidly evaporating by early 1868, the convention was grinding to a halt. Republican delegates took advantage of any possible excuse to leave Albany; even Greeley "vacated his seat sometime before the final adjournment."[27]

As Republicans fled the convention, the Democratic minority found its voice. Several downstate delegates who had been silent for much of the previous year's proceedings now assumed leading roles. Abraham Lawrence, leader of the Apollo Hall Democratic Club in Manhattan, addressed the delegates for the first time on January 28 and offered up an urban Democratic response to the debates of 1867. Addressing the Report of the Committee on Cities, which had endorsed the Citizens' Association's program of unelected commissions, Lawrence asked that upstate delegates recognize the political equality of city residents with rural New Yorkers. The Apollo Hall leader proceeded to dispute the Citizens' Association's legitimacy, claiming that even their name "is a misnomer . . . That Association have never elected a single candidate for a general office . . . their name imports more than the facts warrant."[28]

Lawrence's partisan anger peaked when he quoted the Citizens' Association president Peter Cooper's claim that "the danger in the city of New York is from the too 'unrestricted use of the ballot box!'" For Lawrence, Cooper's statement pointed to the "whole trouble" with municipal reformers. At its heart, Lawrence argued, the 1868 debate was the age-old struggle between "aristocracy and democracy." Of course, his staunch defense of self-rule for urban New Yorkers did not prevent him from voting for separate submission and opposing African American suffrage.[29]

With Democrats clearly in the ascendancy, Republican delegates acquiesced on February 28 to the submission of separate referenda. The convention agreed to put the new constitution to a popular vote in November 1869, at which time voters would decide on three separate questions: the constitution as a whole, a separate judiciary article, and the removal of the property qualifications for African American men. This granted New Yorkers almost two full years to debate the question of black suffrage.

During the months after the constitutional convention concluded in the winter of 1868, the New York City Democratic Party reached the peak of its postbellum powers. As 1868 ended and 1869 began, William M. Tweed cemented his rule over Tammany Hall. John Hoffman was elected governor in 1868. By 1870, Tammany control had moved upstate to the legislature in Albany, resulting in a new municipal charter that was far more favorable to Tammany.

Early in 1868, Samuel J. Tilden began mapping out a party strategy for the 1868 state and national elections. In a letter addressed to other Democratic leaders in New York City, Tilden advised that above all else "our position must be *condemnation and reversal of negro supremacy*," by which the state party chairman meant the adamant denial to African Americans of equal citizenship and impartial suffrage. In a particularly frank explanation of Democratic strategy in Reconstruction-era New York City, Tilden reminded his co-partisans:

> On no other issue can we be so unanimous among ourselves. On no other question can we draw so much from the other side and from the doubtful. It appeals . . . to the adopted citizens—whether Irish or Germans; to all the workingmen; to the young men just becoming voters.

For the remainder of the decade, the city and state Democratic Party heeded its chair's advice and waged a permanent campaign against equal citizenship for African American New Yorkers.[30]

Democrat Horatio Seymour's 1868 presidential campaign brought local New York understandings of Reconstruction to a national audience. Indeed, a New Yorker was the Democratic Party's candidate in each national campaign of the Reconstruction era. Adding to the city's dominant position in the national party, Tammany Hall hosted the national nominating convention during the first week of July. A coalition of New Yorkers and Southerners dominated the July convention, with Republican broadsides estimating that nearly a quarter of all delegates had served in either the Confederate army or Jefferson Davis's administration. Seymour's fall campaign centered around the fight against racial equality. John Van Evrie, editor of the white supremacist *Day Book* and a campaign strategist, advised Seymour to attack Republicans as seeking Reconstruction "on a mongrel basis." Seymour picked up on Van Evrie's suggestions and protested African American political equality as merely a pretense for miscegenation. An engraved portrait of the interracial Louisiana state legislature was considered his most effective propaganda tool: New York City's Democratic newspapers and weeklies often reprinted "the Louisiana engraving," depicting the black majority at work in Baton Rouge, while the party's Philadelphia leadership was "clamorous" for copies and thousands were sent off to Connecticut partisans.[31]

Although Seymour lost the presidency to Ulysses Grant, the former governor of New York garnered over 70 percent of the vote in Manhattan. In the process, John Hoffman gained the governorship and inaugurated an era of emboldened Democratic activism in Empire State politics. In his first address as governor on January 5, 1869, Hoffman brought the party of Seymour and Tilden into a new era. The struggle against the

Fourteenth Amendment was now over; in its place, Hoffman promised a resolute stand against black suffrage in New York and across the nation. The new governor accepted the highest office of the leading state in the Union by denouncing the proposed Fifteenth Amendment to the U.S. Constitution.

In many ways, the second founding was one ongoing political campaign with New York City as its epicenter. Across the nation, local elections were held nearly year-round and repeatedly the terms of debate echoed those of New York. Similar referenda were often on several states' ballots over the course of a single year, and state after state became embroiled in the process of holding a constitutional convention. The political pamphlets from the period rival in number if not in the originality of the ideas those of the Revolutionary War era. For more than a decade after the Civil War, the nation, led by the metropolis, waged the country's first permanent political campaign.

The 1869 struggle over African American manhood suffrage echoed, in many ways, the earlier campaigns of 1846 and 1860 against property qualifications. The same issues were debated and many of the same arguments were advanced. The people of New York State had been debating the specific question since at least June 1867, when the Greeley Committee issued its report. For thirty months, the property qualification was at the center of New York politics. Once 1869 arrived, organizing began in earnest early. By early summer numerous July Fourth orations touched on the question. August witnessed the party conventions, followed in September by Democratic victories in the state elections in the Midwest. The campaign reached a climax in October and early November, but didn't fully conclude until Manhattan's December municipal elections.

For New York African Americans, the 1869 struggle for

suffrage began on January 13 in Washington, D.C. At the National Convention of the Colored Men of America, Manhattan's black leadership—both religious and secular—argued for
a radically universal understanding of equality. Led by the
Rev. J. Sella Martin, the New York delegation broke ranks
with the rest of the convention and demanded equal ad-
mission for women. Sella argued that "it was a convention
of men, and the term 'men' in the Bible meant men and
women." The New Yorkers' primary concern at the convention was the issue of equal suffrage for all citizens. On January 15, H. C. Moulson of New York issued the convention's
most stirring call for equal suffrage. Starting with an invocation of Jefferson's ideals, Moulson called on Reconstruction-
era Americans to live up to the nation's founding ideals.
Meaningful equality, for Moulson and the New York delegation, required race-blind suffrage.[32]

Empire State African Americans intensified their work on
behalf of suffrage reform throughout 1869. In March, the
Central Committee of New York State Colored Citizens issued a "Call for a State Convention." New York black activists hoped that after a half century the 1821 restrictions
would at last be removed. On the afternoon of June 1, the
Convention of Colored Men of New York State assembled at
the Academy of Music in Binghamton; immediately the delegates focused their energies on the coming fall campaign for
equal suffrage.[33] Remarkably, at what was the most critical of
all African American state conventions of the postwar decade,
the Binghamton convention's preeminent speaker was a black
woman, Maud Molson. After pledging loyalty to the Republican Party and running through a range of theoretical ideas
about race, Molson turned to the Democratic Party's constant
"cry of the white man's government." Molson explained to

the audience that whenever she heard such talk, she immediately thought of the Indians "who occupied the land long before the white man was here." With regard to Manhattan's white supremacist politicians, the Binghamton assembly recognized that the New York City Democratic Party posed the greatest obstacle to the achievement of long-desired suffrage reform.[34]

In New York City and across the state, the leadership of the fall campaign for equal manhood suffrage was largely composed of African American ministers. Rev. William F. Butler, of Manhattan's African Methodist Episcopal Church, led scores of his colleagues in organizing from the pulpit, appealing to their black congregations while also addressing white Protestants. In October, the ministers issued "An Appeal to Christians," in which they couched their demand for black equality in religious language. Asking all congregations in Manhattan to reserve Sunday, October 31, for special sermons on the meaning and necessity of equal citizenship, Butler and his colleagues argued for an equality rooted in Christian fellowship. Their final appeal before the November election and the separate referenda ended with a warning: "He who rejects our prayer virtually proclaims that there is no right and no wrong in politics, and that the rule of the strongest is the law of society and the mandate of heaven." Manhattan's black clergymen sought to advance the cause of political equality and, in the process, moralize the realm of politics.[35]

Not all African American organizing in late 1869 New York City centered around local churches. That fall witnessed the movement on the part of hundreds of black workers and reformers to form the New York City Labor Council, a new workingmen's group opposed to the racial exclusions of the city's mainstream labor organizations. Meeting regularly throughout the fall campaign season, the group's member-ship—men and women, mostly laborers with a few physicians and clergymen—linked the short-term struggle for suffrage to a longer-term fight for economic and political reform. Along-side the right to vote, the council asserted "the right to labor." Among a wide range of other reforms, the council demanded jobs, land reform, and cooperative workshops. Recognizing the "power which the spirit of slavery and caste still holds over the minds of our white fellow citizen," the city's secular black activists embraced a politics of equal citizenship alert to the complicated intersections of race and class in the postwar metropolis.

In the last week before the election to be held on No-vember 2, tempers flared across the city. Thirty months of debate over race and suffrage now escalated to the point of vio-lence. Democratic rallies overflowed with rabidly antiblack speeches. Problack suffrage supporters, at the same time, grew bolder in their public appeals. In the process, few white Manhattanites rallied to the cause of equal manhood suffrage. On Friday night, October 29, just four days before the elec-tion, two African American ministers were savagely stoned and beaten on Hudson Street. Reverends William F. Butler and Jacob Thomson, two leaders of the struggle for black suf-frage, narrowly escaped death.[36]

On November 2, the Radical Republican era in New York state politics came to an end with another defeat of equal manhood suffrage. In Manhattan, black suffrage was defeated by a vote of 65,189 to 27,390. The Democratic Party capital-ized on the opposition to interracial democracy, capturing both houses of the state legislature. The high optimism with which William A. Wheeler had opened the convention of 1867–1868 had long since vanished.[37]

Meanwhile, two hundred miles to the south in Washington, D.C., congressional Republicans were following events in the nation's state capitals. One by one, state legislatures were ratifying the proposed Fifteenth Amendment to the U.S. Constitution. As 1869 ended, the new amendment—guaranteeing equal manhood suffrage—neared the requisite approval of three-quarters of the states. In Manhattan, 1870 would witness a historic struggle between national constitutional revision and enduring local attachments to a racially restricted political order.

5

ACTS OF ENFORCEMENT

The year 1870 was a critical one in the second founding's long history. With the enactment of the Fifteenth Amendment and the first two Enforcement Acts, the Republican president and Congress embarked on a reform agenda that eclipsed previous postbellum measures in the extent and nature of its nationwide impact. Centered around suffrage and federal power, this new stage of Reconstruction focused as much on New York City as on any other locality. Manhattan's election of 1870, the city's first based on equal manhood suffrage, required federal action to ensure black men their right to vote. At the same time, the constitutional protection afforded by the Reconstruction Amendments empowered Republican Party officials in New York to launch an unparalleled process of federal regulation of urban elections. A mixture of idealism and centralism fueled the federal reconstruction of New York City in 1870, resulting in a transformed political landscape for the remainder of the Gilded Age. Nowhere is the nationalization of Reconstruction in the wake of the Fifteenth Amendment's enactment more in evidence than in New York City's fall 1870 election.[1]

To understand that election season, we must come to terms with the Enforcement Acts, which created a federal bureaucracy responsible for guaranteeing fair and equal elections. The 1870 election in New York City set a precedent, both locally and nationally, for the next quarter century. Through 1894, tens of thousands of federal officials oversaw elections in New York City and in other major metropolitan areas. For much of the Gilded Age, the most visible federal presence in the nation's cities came every two years on Election Day. Historians of urban politics have too often underplayed the significance of the federal government's role in Northern urban life in the last third of the nineteenth century.[2] The vast majority of all federal spending on the regulation of elections was spent in the North, with nearly half going to the cities of New York State. Beginning in 1870, over 25 percent of federal enforcement expenditures were directed at one municipality: New York City.[3]

While in early 1870 Tammany Democrats remained adamantly opposed to the new amendment, other New Yorkers, including a number of Republicans, took the position that with enfranchisement Reconstruction was now complete. E. L. Godkin editorialized in the *Nation* that with the ratification of the Fifteenth Amendment, "the reconstruction process may now be considered closed for all practical purposes."[4] Horace Greeley's *Tribune* hailed "the completion of the good work of their Emancipation."[5] Even the American Anti-Slavery Society, which had remained in operation for the first five years after the Civil War, resolved to disband on April 9, the day after the amendment's enactment. A widespread sense of closure, verging on self-satisfaction, characterized mainstream metropolitan sentiment on questions of racial justice in the early months of 1870.

In opposition to such an interpretation, other New Yorkers came forward to define enfranchisement as but a necessary and far-from-final step in the reconstruction of the North. Unlike earlier commemorations of victories won for Southern blacks, the numerous meetings organized by black New Yorkers in the first months of 1870 now emphasized the struggle for racial justice in the North. To celebrate enfranchisement, African American New Yorkers prepared a mass celebration of the amendment's ratification for April 8. In the weeks leading up to the celebration, there were numerous organized gatherings in the metropolitan black community, most held at local houses of worship. A reporter at a late March planning meeting remarked that, "I have never seen an assemblage more full of joy—exuberant joy."[6] Less than six months after New Yorkers had rejected a state constitutional amendment guaranteeing equal manhood suffrage, black New Yorkers understood that it was the federal government that was guaranteeing their right to vote.

On April 8, black Manhattanites commemorated the adoption of the Fifteenth Amendment with a mass parade down Broadway, from Thirty-fourth Street to Union Square. Over fifteen thousand onlookers—men and women, mostly black—lined the parade route. The seven thousand marchers were all African American men. Parading behind a banner that read "We Ask Nothing But a Fair Race in Life," the assembled veterans' groups, military clubs, and benevolent associations celebrated the elevation of black men to equal citizenship.[7] That evening, Rev. Henry Highland Garnet addressed a mass meeting at Cooper Institute, reminding his audience that the vote was not a "universal panacea for all our woes, our social difficulties and troubles . . . it has only given us fair play." The first Enforcement Act had yet to pass, but Garnet, calling for further federal legislation to make real the promise of enfranchisement, anticipated the need. In April and May 1870, Garnet and other leading black Manhattanites supported the Republicans in their struggle to enact the Enforcement Acts. Across the nation, Republicans viewed the first Enforcement Act—which would provide the legal and administrative basis for full civil rights—as essential to realizing the ideals of democratic citizenship regardless of race.[8]

At the same time, supporters of the first Enforcement Act of May 31, 1870, were especially driven by worries over corruption in local Northern municipal politics. Fraudulent voting in Manhattan had been a worry since at least the first decades of the century.[9] In the 1860s, the Republican Party seized on this concern, particularly after the 1868 election had highlighted the problem and led to partisan action. In a process that would be repeated throughout the Gilded Age, a local metropolitan elite was able to initiate federal legislation, which would affect both New York and the rest of the nation. The Union League Club of New York—the Republican Party's organizational home in the city—began investigating the 1868 frauds in October, even before Election Day. U.S. Marshal Murray testified to club lawyers as to the extensive naturalization frauds being practiced in the city's courtrooms. Another investigator testified to being able to buy naturalization papers for "two dollars apiece" in a basement "lager-bier saloon" at 6 Centre Street.[10] And it was alleged that in two weeks that October Municipal Court Judge George G. Barnard naturalized over ten thousand new citizens all on his own.[11]

A month after the 1868 election, the Union League Club

submitted a memorandum to the U.S. Congress demanding immediate action. In short order, the House of Representatives established a Committee to Investigate the Alleged New York City Election Frauds under the leadership of William Lawrence, a Republican from Ohio. The committee, dominated by Republicans and composed entirely of representatives from rural districts, set to work in the winter of 1868–1869.[12] John Davenport, a twenty-five-year-old Republican lawyer for the New York Union League Club, was appointed clerk and led the Lawrence Committee through months of testimony in Washington, D.C., and Manhattan.[13] The committee's report deemed New York City's 1868 election fraudulent, "the result of a systematic plan of gigantic proportions, stealthily prearranged and boldly executed."[14] Republicans in Congress made special note of the extraordinarily high number of naturalizations registered in Manhattan courtrooms in the summer and fall of 1868. The committee recommended a number of sweeping changes in the nation's election and naturalization laws, many of which would become part of the Enforcement Acts.

One year later, on May 31, 1870, the Forty-first Congress enacted the first Enforcement Act. This "act to enforce the Right of Citizens of the United States to Vote in the several States of this Union, and for other purposes" was the first of several pieces of historic legislation designed to guarantee the protections of the Fourteenth and Fifteenth Amendments. The act's first eighteen provisions tackled a range of pressing concerns: the implementation of the recently enacted Fifteenth Amendment, the creation of a federal enforcement bureaucracy, the enforcement of the equal protection clause of the Fourteenth Amendment, and the reenactment of certain provisions of the Civil Rights Act of 1866.[15] Two additional sections of the act, sections 19 and 20, however, were almost identical to the proposals outlined in the 1869 report of the Lawrence Committee.[16] These two sections made certain acts, if committed in congressional elections, federal crimes; lawmakers targeted such practices as individuals voting multiple times, false registration, and preventing eligible voters from casting a ballot.[17]

In the House, Rep. John Bingham, author of the Fourteenth Amendment, drafted an initial enforcement act with only the first eighteen sections. It was in the Senate that sections 19 and 20 were added. Republican Senator Sherman from Ohio promoted his two additional sections, claiming "there is one other grievance that I feel ought to be dealt with at this moment . . . a grievance which has become of greater magnitude even than the denial of the right to vote to colored people; and that is, the open, glaring, admitted frauds by wholesale in the great cities of this country."[18] In case anyone needed further clarification, Sherman defined the recent events in New York City as "a national evil so great, so dangerous, and so alarming in its character, that it is the duty of Congress to protect itself and the people . . ."[19] Here, Sherman signaled a dramatic shift in the priorities of the national Republican Party; for the remainder of the second founding and throughout the Gilded Age, the reconstruction of New York City was viewed as no less imperative than the reconstruction of the South.

In the late spring and early summer of 1870, events continued to unfold in Washington, D.C., that would have a decisive impact on the November election in New York City. In June, Congress authorized the creation of the Department of Justice, thereby establishing an organizational apparatus for implementing the numerous provisions of the first Enforce-

ment Act. And on July 14, Congress passed a Naturalization
Act, directed at preventing the electoral abuses that had been
carried out in New York City in 1868; also known as the Elections Act, this was the second Enforcement Act.[20]

The New York Union League Club had been arguing for
naturalization reform since early 1869. In January of that year,
the club sent a second memorandum to Congress on the scale
of the naturalization frauds perpetrated in New York City in
1868, and demanded substantial changes in the process by
which an immigrant became a citizen. Throughout the nineteenth century, any court—federal, state, or municipal—was
empowered to naturalize new citizens. The club's 1869 memorandum recommended that Congress federalize this process
and strip local and state courts of the power to naturalize.

On June 13, 1870, Rep. Noah Davis, a New York Republican and himself a leading member of the Union League
Club, introduced a bill to reform the nation's naturalization
laws. The Senate responded quickly with a different bill, one
much more focused on New York's City's particular problems.
Section 6 of the Senate bill would have invalidated all naturalization certificates issued in Manhattan after July 1868.
Section 12 called for the appointment of federal election supervisors for all cities with populations over twenty thousand,
while section 13 provided for the appointment of special federal deputy marshals to patrol polling places on the day of national elections.

A Republican from New York, Sen. Roscoe Conkling, was
the primary supporter of these sections. Appealing for support, Conkling declared that these three sections were "most
important in my state," where, he stated "the Republican
party in the state of New York . . . is year after year defrauded
of the free and honest expression of the majority of the peo-

ple of the great Commonwealth by frauds which smell to high heaven."[21] In the end, after negotiations between the House and the Senate, the final Naturalization Act was passed; of Conkling's three proposed sections, only section 6 was removed. In its final form, the law authorized "special deputy marshals" and gave them "power to make arrests without warrants."[22]

With this second Enforcement Act on the books, there was no mistaking the Republican Party's national ambitions. The legislation targeted only those cities with populations over twenty thousand. Of the sixty-eight American communities of such size in 1870, only ten were in the former Confederacy.[23] Federal concern for suffrage reform was now focused on the urban North as much as on the rural South.

Following the legislative flurry of the late spring and early summer, federal officials in Manhattan were left to scramble to implement the complex new regulatory apparatus in time for November's congressional elections. One reason for the intense national interest in New York's electoral contest was that John Hoffman, former Tammany mayor, was running for reelection as governor. Republicans feared that this popular Democrat would challenge President Grant nationally in 1872.[24] In this partisan atmosphere, local Republican Party officials and appointees took the lead in manning the newly created positions of U.S. supervisors of elections and deputy marshals.

John I. Davenport led the Republican Party's attempt to regulate the 1870 election. His career represented the mixture of partisan fervor and postbellum idealism that characterized the national Republican Party's enactment of the first two En-

In the weeks after the Draft Riots, the metropolitan press struggled to come to terms with what had happened. This image from *Frank Leslie's Illustrated Newspaper* depicts one lynching from the third night of the violence. ("Scene in Thirty-Second Street . . ." *Frank Leslie's Illustrated Newspaper.* August 1, 1863, American Social History Project, New York)

New Yorkers came together to mourn Lincoln's death on April 24, 1865. Just two weeks after the Civil War's end, thousands of Manhattanites gathered at City Hall for the fallen president's funeral procession. (Negative #21184, Collection of The New-York Historical Society)

"THIS IS A WHITE MAN'S GOVERNMENT."

"We regard the Reconstruction Acts (so called) of Congress as usurpations, and unconstitutional, revolutionary, and void."—*Democratic Platform.*

Thomas Nast completed this sketch in the aftermath of the 1868 Democratic National Convention at Tammany Hall. A Five Points Irishman, the ex-confederate and Ku Klux Klan founder Nathan Bedford Forrest, and the Wall Street financier and Democratic supporter August Belmont stand atop an African American veteran, with the Colored Orphan's Asylum burning in the background. (*Harper's Weekly*, September 5, 1868. Reprinted by permission of the President and Fellows of Harvard College)

African American men who would serve as U.S. deputy marshals and election officials take the oath of office, dramatizing the profound transformations of New York's second founding. (*Frank Leslie's Illustrated Newspaper*, November 19, 1870. Reprinted by permission of the President and Fellows of Harvard College)

Collective violence persisted throughout the Reconstruction years in Manhattan. Here, the police attack radical and working-class protesters in
Tompkins Square in January 1874. (*Frank Leslie's Illustrated Newspaper*, January 31, 1874.

In the weeks leading up to the 1876 presidential election, Thomas Nast sought to discredit Samuel J. Tilden by recalling the New York governor's less-than-loyal behavior during the Civil War. Caught between North and South, Tilden personified New York City's position in national political life in the postbellum era. (*Harper's Weekly*, October 14, 1876. Reprinted by permission of the President and Fellows of Harvard College)

Looking west from the Brooklyn tower of the unfinished Brooklyn Bridge in the centennial year of 1876, this panoramic vista suggests a city caught between past and future as the second founding came to an end. (Negative # 32185, Collection of The New-York Historical Society)

Turn-of-the-century New Yorkers invoked the memory of the second founding once more at the 1897 dedication of Grant's Tomb, high above the Hudson River at 122nd Street and Riverside Drive. (Library of Congress, Prints and Photographs Division, LC-USZ62-70534)

forcement Acts. Born in Brooklyn in 1843, Davenport joined the Union army during the Civil War, serving as a top aide under both Benjamin Butler and Ulysses S. Grant. In the last months of the war, the young New Yorker was head of the Bureau of Information of the Army of the James, employing scouts and spies to compile a thorough account of the activities and power of Lee's army.[25] Davenport also had worked under Butler overseeing Manhattan polling places in the fall 1864 election. Davenport's military experiences would inform his approach to his work as federal election supervisor for Manhattan in the last three decades of the nineteenth century.

With the war's end, the twenty-two-year-old New Yorker spent several years building connections in the national Republic Party. In rapid succession, Davenport served as clerk in Washington to New York Sen. Edwin D. Morgan, assisted Carl Schurz in founding the *Detroit Post*, and returned home to work for Horace Greeley's *New York Tribune*. He had barely settled into a private legal practice in 1868 before he threw himself into the work of documenting that year's election frauds for the Union League Club.[26] Davenport not only served as counsel to both the club and the Lawrence Committee, he was also the primary author of the Enforcement Acts' provisions regarding Northern elections, which directly led U.S. Judge Lewis B. Woodruff to appoint Davenport as U.S. commissioner in September 1870 with responsibility to prevent fraudulent registrations in Manhattan.[27]

Davenport committed himself to the work. In October, he successfully lobbied President Grant to issue an executive order allowing government officials in New York City to grant ten-day leaves of absence to all workers to "register and vote at the November elections."[28] Hundreds of these federal office holders served as election supervisors or deputy marshals.

The administration in Washington, D.C., focused much of its attention that fall on preparations for the New York election.[29] In the month leading up to Election Day, 90 percent of all Department of Justice communications concerned Northern enforcement of the Fifteenth Amendment.[30]

As rumors of possible violence at the polls spread around the city, Davenport's colleague U.S. Marshal George Sharpe wrote to his superiors in Washington:

> The *World* . . . contains editorial articles in its issues . . . which are calculated in its own language to "provoke the people to go to the polls with arms in their hands." If the intent intended by these articles be produced, a class of armed men will be found at the polls on the days of registration and election who may overawe the United States officers in the performance of their duties if not provided with the means of defending their person . . . I respectfully ask that the deputies to be appointed may be afforded the reasonable protection.[31]

Attorney General Amos T. Akerman immediately wired his reply, alerting Sharpe that military officials in New York had been advised to provide the marshals with all necessary arms.[32] Local papers speculated as to which general would come to New York to lead the federal presence. One especially troubling report suggested that it would be General Terry, who had recently been stationed in the South overseeing military rule of the former Confederacy.[33]

By the last week of October, federal officials in New York had appointed nearly eight hundred supervisors and twelve hundred marshals. John Davenport spent the days leading up to the election hurriedly swearing in hundreds of deputy marshals in great secrecy.[34] The most noteworthy dimension of this rapidly created federal force was its interracial composition. The *Evening Post* was but one of several metropolitan dailies that noted in its late October columns the numbers of black men appointed as U.S. deputy marshals in New York: "A large number of colored men were among the special deputies sworn in."[35] By early November, at least two hundred black deputy marshals had been sworn in, marking a dramatic departure in the character of federal authority on the city's streets.[36]

The swearing in of African American federal marshals coincided with the widespread political mobilization of black Manhattan in the fall of 1870. Local activists had met continuously since the spring's celebrations of the Fifteenth Amendment's ratification. Urban delegates dominated the State Convention of Colored Voters in Syracuse.[37] In New York City, agitation in preparation for the coming election began in earnest in early October. On Monday, October 10, at the corner of Broad and Wall streets, a group of black New Yorkers proclaimed the following resolution: "The peace and safety of the city and State of New York are placed in jeopardy by [the municipal government] in their desperate war against the honest discharge of the elective franchise."[38] This warning was issued on the very day that Marshal Sharpe was petitioning the attorney general for military support.

Manhattan's black community was entering a new era in the fall of 1870. The city's first equal manhood suffrage election coincided with an important demographic shift. After the historic decline of the black population in New York City in the mid-1860s, an interesting reversal began around 1870; for the first time since the draft riots of 1863, New York's African American population began to rise. Barely a decade removed from the horrors of July 1863, the city's black community experienced a historic wave of in-migration in the early 1870s, with a rate of population growth double that of white New Yorkers.[39] A range of factors led to this surge of black migration from the upper South to the city, from the impact of Klan terror to encouragement from Freedman's Bureau operatives. This migration did not by any means signify that New York City was a newfound beacon of racial justice in the 1870s. However, the metropolis—because of its promise of employment and the possibility of the vote for men—was now one of the best of a range of increasingly bad options for African Americans from the rural South.[40]

Amid this resurgent black community, the black deputy marshals appearing on the streets of Manhattan in late October and early November of 1870 carried real and symbolic power. The Democratic press, led by the *New York World*, spread numerous allegations against the deputy marshals, and Tammany supporters took a special delight in running through the alleged criminal pasts of several African American deputy marshals.[41] The *Sun* sarcastically noted the "swearing in [of] the Model Supervisors," claiming that the worst of this "very large gang of ruffians" were from the interracial Eighth Ward, center of the metropolitan black community.[42]

Pressure on the black deputy marshals did not come solely from the local Democratic press. The Tammany-controlled police department directed its forces against the black community of lower Manhattan and particularly against the agents of the federal government. A wave of police-initiated arrests and violence in late October was centered in Manhattan's Eighth Ward. On Halloween night, ten black men were arrested at an "eating house" on Grand Street. The following night brought the arrest of fourteen more African Americans at a downtown billiard saloon. November 2 saw two black men arrested in front of their home on Thompson Street. Nearly all those arrested were charged with vagrancy or presence in a disorderly house.[43]

A number of the arrests made in the downtown black community on October 31 coincided with a meeting of "the colored citizens of the Sixth District" on lower Sixth Avenue that night.[44] Police actions regularly followed such African American public meetings in the Eighth Ward, and the arrest of a black federal officer in the days before the election greatly intensified anxieties. Local Eighth Precinct police arrested Charles Wilson as he walked down Broome Street. Wilson, recently appointed a special deputy U.S. marshal, later reported that the arresting officer boasted that the police "are going to arrest all of you nigger marshals."[45] True to the threat, numerous other black special deputy marshals were arrested in the final two weeks before the election on November 8.[46]

Federal officials, led by Commissioner Davenport, issued a warrant for the capture of the officer who had arrested Wilson and for Police Justice John Cox. Davenport indicted Cox on charges that he had "comprised and [conspired] to obstruct the operation of the United States law by intimidating the colored deputy marshals of the 8th Ward, by arresting them on false charges."[47] Cox and two Eighth Precinct officers were eventually arrested, but not until November 9, the day after the election.[48] Once Cox was committed to the Ludlow Street Jail, he was quickly bailed out by "Boss" Tweed; leading Tammany officials were responsible for bailing out several of those arrested by Davenport in early November.[49]

In late October, Davenport had succeeded in impaneling a grand jury to focus on violations of the Enforcement Acts. He quickly issued thirty warrants for false registration, and federal officers made five arrests on October 18, the first day of registration. Terence Quinn, a convicted felon, and John McLaughlin, secretary of the Tammany Hall General Committee, were two of the earliest arrests. Davenport's initial targets were typical of his ensuing arrests in the fall of 1870. Quinn, who had served time for manslaughter, stood as a clear symbol of Irish criminality. McLaughlin, the first of several Tammany officials whom Davenport would prosecute, revealed the extent of the local Democratic Party's wrongdoing.[50]

It was the Quinn case that had the greatest impact both locally and nationally. Quinn's lawyers, led by the eminent jurist George Ticknor Curtis, quickly filed a demurrer, arguing against the constitutionality of the two Enforcement Acts of 1870. At this point, President Grant took a special interest in the case, sending his personal counsel Caleb Cushing to Manhattan to assist the U.S. attorney in countering Curtis's motion.[51] Presiding Judge Woodruff oversaw a rapid sequence of arguments and rebuttals on November 1 and 2 and proceeded to deliver his opinion in the case of *United States v. Quinn* on November 3. The promptness of the court's finding, Woodruff explained, reflected that he "entertain[ed] no doubt" as to the constitutionality of the Election Law of 1870.[52] For the first half of the 1870s, the Quinn case set an important precedent, allowing federal officials great power in prosecuting fraudulent registration and voting.[53]

With Woodruff's decision in favor of Davenport's office, federal officials felt there was a growing sense of control in Manhattan during the week leading up to Election Day. By early November, Manhattanites noted the increased military presence. The sloop of war *Guerriere* was docked in the East River to receive accused illegal voters. General

McDowell placed the soldiers in the Department of the East under Marshal Sharpe's—and by extension John Davenport's—command.[54] George Templeton Strong, the Republican lawyer, was positively ecstatic at the display of federal might. As November 8 neared, he wrote in his diary that "an outbreak on a large scale, thoroughly repressed and followed by a month of martial law judiciously administered might do New York much good."[55]

Faced with the historic mobilization of the federal government's legal and military power, New York City's Democracy struggled to respond. Building on Peter Sweeny's earlier attack on the Fifteenth Amendment as merely a means of centralization, Tammany leaders devoted the fall campaign to attacking the Enforcement Acts and Davenport's administration of those acts. William M. Tweed closed down Tammany Hall's grand preelection spectacle on October 27 with a rousing condemnation of the Republican Party's "invasion" of New York. Tweed concluded his remarks by warning his co-partisans that "the oppressor's hand . . . is upon our throat."[56] James Kelso, Tammany's newly appointed police superintendent, issued an order in late October that while his men should try to cooperate with federal officials, "the access for voters to the polls must be kept open and unobstructed."[57] On November 7, the afternoon before the election, Kelso swore in eighteen hundred special policemen, with the specific intent of countering the federal presence at the polls.[58]

In the buildup to Election Day, all sides worried over the possibility of mass violence. The *Journal of Commerce* warned of a "federal invasion of New York," claiming that the president had "ordered to New York all the available soldiers and marines east of the Mississippi."[59] The city police ordered all officers on duty for the entire polling day on November 8.[60]

After several days of bitter negotiations, local authorities and federal officials brokered an uneasy truce late in the afternoon on November 7: U.S. marshals were to be stationed inside polling places, while at least two New York City police officers would stand guard outside.[61]

On Election Day itself, six thousand deputy marshals and twenty-five hundred police oversaw the ballot boxes.[62] In the day's early hours, the election's most noteworthy feature seemed to be the presence of African Americans at the polls. One journalist noted that "the most popular man was the new-made citizen—the colored man . . . An unusual number of negroes were on the street: and in one or two districts they distributed the tickets."[63] As the day went on, however, rumors of riots raced around the city and the nation. The Washington correspondent for the *Evening Post* reported that word had reached the nation's capital of a brawl between the New York National Guard and U.S. troops.[64] The Eighth Ward, as had been predicted, turned out to be the most explosive area in Manhattan. Through the morning hours and into the early afternoon, several blacks were arrested for repeat voting, though no whites were. At 2:45 p.m., George W. Francis, an African American special deputy marshal, was arrested inside a polling place by Eighth Precinct police for "creating a disturbance." Word of the arrest spread through the west Manhattan neighborhood and a large crowd of local blacks surrounded the police. With that, Capt. McDonnell "decided that the officers had exceeded their duty, and ordered Francis to be set at liberty."[65]

A "general melee" between special policemen and deputy marshals at Seventeenth Street and Ninth Avenue occurred; there were also reports of violence in the Thirteenth Ward. U.S. Deputy Marshal Jacob Healy was taking a prisoner to the station house when he was attacked by a mob and severely wounded. In the resulting chaos, Healy discharged his revolver and wounded Jacob Vetter; he became the only U.S. marshal arrested by Tenth Precinct police.[66] Elsewhere, Deputy Marshal P. J. O'Brien was stopped while arresting William Craven at the corner of East Broadway and Market Street. A crowd surrounded O'Brien and a revolver was pointed at the marshal; in the chaos, the prisoner escaped. Numerous such instances of confronting federal authority, either with violence or its threat, took place that Election Day.[67]

In spite of the threats and violence, the fears of a large-scale confrontation never materialized. And despite the federal presence, the state Democratic Party won another major victory, with John Hoffman reelected governor for a second two-year term. "Boss" Tweed and his Tammany Hall colleagues managed to tighten their control over both municipal and state governments, in large measure due to their successful attacks on federal centralization and the "invasion of New York."[68]

Their electoral defeat of November 1870 only encouraged the national Republican Party to intensify the federal regulation of elections in the coming months. In February 1871, Congress passed a new Enforcement Act that built directly on the Naturalization Act of July 1870. The new law regularized the duties of supervisors and marshals, setting precise standards as to their location, duties, and powers. This new legislation sought to nationalize John Davenport's techniques for use in other municipalities. President Grant signed it on February 28; two days later, he telegraphed Davenport at the Union League Club: "Election bill signed day before yesterday. Regret that I forgot to telegraph you sooner."[69]

The fourth Enforcement Act, also called the Ku Klux Klan

Act, went into force in April 1871. Aimed at prosecuting the Klan's first wave of terror throughout the South, this law represented the most heroic dimensions of President Grant's approach to Reconstruction. The law gave the attorney general the power to assign hundreds of U.S. marshals and Justice Department lawyers throughout the former Confederacy to track down the Klan and protect the rights of freedpeople.[70] Grant's Justice Department vigorously enforced the act's provisions and succeeded in suppressing the first incarnation of the Klan. As part of the federal commitment to restoring order in the South, the Forty-second Congress in 1871 allocated fifty thousand dollars as a Secret Service fund to be used at the discretion of the attorney general.

Between 1871 and 1876, nearly 70 percent of that money was directed to John Davenport's office in New York City.[71] President Grant, Davenport, and the national Republican leadership viewed the regulation of municipal elections in New York as an essential part of any continued Reconstruction program. The only way to protect black rights in the South, they reasoned, was by electing Republicans in the North. Grant maintained a deep interest in Davenport's work throughout his second term, meeting with him on his many visits to Manhattan. Attorney General George H. Williams recalled in 1876 that "the President seemed to think that Mr. Davenport was doing a very great work in New York."[72] Davenport's power correspondingly extended broadly through various areas of the Gilded Age state. In the centennial year, the chief supervisor of elections also served as U.S. commissioner and as clerk of the U.S. Circuit Court.[73]

The federal supervision of elections strengthened the Republican presence in the nation's metropolis. During the next quarter century of federal regulation of elections,

Manhattan was targeted more than any other municipality throughout the country. Between 1870 and 1894, 27 percent of federal spending on the election supervisors and deputy marshals was allocated to the Southern District of New York.[74] The nation's leading city experienced a militarization of social relations in the last decades of the nineteenth century that was paralleled by a contemporaneous militarization of the ballot box. Both the federal government and even more the New York City police stepped up their presence in the weeks leading up to congressional elections. As late as 1892, there were eight thousand special deputy marshals in New York City on Election Day.[75]

6

LIBERTY AND THE POSTWAR CITY

As the city's black population increased for the first time since the bloody days of July 1863, New York City held out the promise of some limited economic and personal liberty to growing numbers of African Americans from the rural North and the Reconstruction-era South. One such migrant, Emma Waite, came to Manhattan from upstate Saratoga in 1870. In Waite's diary, a breathless embrace of the freedoms of urban life was balanced by a constant recognition of the special exclusions faced by black Manhattanites. It wasn't her first time in the city. During the 1860s, Waite lived downstate for brief periods, but she had always felt like an outsider. Home was Saratoga, where she mixed domestic work with employment at the grand resort hotels and resided amid a large, permanent, and seemingly secure community of African Americans. There, in the first months of 1870, Waite had attended lectures by Frederick Douglass and by Henry Highland Garnet, and participated in the local celebration of the enactment of the Fifteenth Amendment. The town's black men and women organized a ball in the spring to commemorate enfranchisement. By summer, however, Waite's optimism faded as she lost several jobs at local hotels "on account of their getting white help." Her situation grew so desperate that by early October she headed south to Manhattan for work.[1]

Waite possessed a complicated understanding of liberty in the nation's metropolis. Like many other African American newcomers arriving in the city in the early 1870s, Emma Waite conveyed a profound ambivalence about urban freedom, describing her world as one of "hopes and disappointments." She quickly became a devoted fan of the city's theatrical culture, developing something of a crush on the actress Lydia Thomson. Work at Apollo Hall afforded Waite the opportunity to listen to near-nightly lectures on a wide range of public issues. The new Manhattanite was swept up in the popular and political culture of the city. Among the most cherished moments noted in her journal of city life was her first payday. November 1870 "Came in very nice"; her pay packet allowed a day's shopping and a night at the theater. Soon, Waite's pride in her economic independence was tempered by her growing recognition of the constraints on her place as a working woman in postbellum New York City. Before the year was out, Waite lost work to allegedly unqualified whites, was forced to work on Thanksgiving and Christmas, and began to consider leaving the city. Her diary entry on the year's last day noted 1870 as "a year of sorrows and disappointments like many others to me."[2]

While Emma Waite gained knowledge of the limits of liberty in the Reconstruction-era city, many African American activists in Manhattan struggled to introduce a seemingly un-American term, *caste*, into metropolitan and national discussions of liberty. Through the early 1870s, talk of caste became a central tool for black New Yorkers to criticize the limitations to black freedom that Emma Waite confronted. Where *liberty* was a preferred term for nearly all New Yorkers, caste remained a keyword only within the city's black communities, intended to address the structural dimensions of Northern racism. Few other New Yorkers were willing to adopt such language in the 1870s, preferring instead to think about race and liberty in terms of individual prejudice.[3]

Defining Liberty

The political order of early Reconstruction came crashing down in the first half of the 1870s as New Yorkers fought to define the meaning of liberty in the wake of suffrage extension and aggressive federal intervention in the life of the city. A remarkably capacious term for New Yorkers in the first years of the seventies, liberty came to represent a wide range of ideas and programs: civil rights, home rule, economic opportunity, personal freedom, laissez-faire, to name only a few. All over Manhattan, a popular debate over the keyword of liberty was joined even amid the enforcement politics of 1870 and would continue on through 1874.[4]

In these years, New Yorkers thought long and hard about the possibilities and paradoxes of freedom in the wake of emancipation and constitutional revision. Just whose liberty needed protection? many New Yorkers asked. What was the proper content of postwar liberty in the nation's metropolis? The transformative impact of national Reconstruction was most deeply felt between 1870 and 1874, as old political alliances were shaken and new forces arose.

In response to the expansive definitions of liberty offered up by Manhattan's African American citizens, an assortment of Liberal Republicans and Democrats mobilized to combat what they perceived to be the crisis of modern mass democracy. Such self-proclaimed "Best Men" were active in both national and local politics, articulating an increasingly assertive rejection of democratic principles. At the heart of their politics was a notion of liberty as laissez-faire, most notably calling for the end of activist government in both the still-reconstructing South and the wards of New York City. For these conservative reformers, liberty was defined in negative terms, as freedom *from* the many dangers of modern urban life: mob rule, centralism, economic regulation.[5]

This laissez-faire understanding of liberty was in turn challenged by increasing numbers of laboring New Yorkers. As the second founding wore on, important elements in the metropolitan working class slowly became radicalized. Culminating in the Tompkins Square "riot" of January 1874, many working New Yorkers slowly moved beyond the "white workingmen's democracy" of the late sixties and advanced a new democratic politics, one founded on a positive sense of liberty, now defined as freedom *to* hold a job, participate in politics, and make claims on the government.[6]

By 1870, "Boss" William M. Tweed controlled the Tammany Hall Democratic organization, and with it all of New York state and city politics. Tweed allies held not only the mayor's office and a majority of seats on the common council and the board of aldermen, but also a controlling influence in both houses of the state legislature and in the person of John Hoffman, the governor's mansion in Albany. As Tweed took control of the state senate in early 1870, his machine's power stretched from Manhattan to Albany and across the state to Lake Erie. He single-handedly occupied the office of state senator, county supervisor, superintendent of public works, grand sachem of Tammany Hall, and supervisor of the county courthouse. Tweed was not surprisingly the prime beneficiary of the new municipal charter for New York City that the legislature passed. With its rule ever more secure, the Tweed organization gained immense control over public works projects across Manhattan.[7]

The brief era of Tweed/Tammany dominance signaled the greatest success of the postwar Democratic Party's white supremacist conception of American liberty. The "sacred but vulnerable liberty" of the American people was under attack, Tammany orators argued, and local sovereignty, or home rule, was necessary in both the South and the urban North. Boss Tweed—and his "ring" of advisors and associates—claimed home rule as the ultimate guarantor of the liberty of New York City residents. Related to this argument, Tweed secured additional funding and independence for the Catholic parochial schools of the city, in the process winning a great deal of Irish Catholic support. For the Boss of bosses, liberty was simply a matter of letting New York City's Democratic leadership rule the metropolis as it saw fit.

Crises of 1871

One short year later, Tweed's seemingly iron hold on state and municipal public life loosened. A series of dramatic crises exploded in Manhattan and elsewhere to transform the city's political cultures. In place of the entrenched racial politics that had characterized metropolitan politics in the last years of the 1860s, three local and international incidents in 1871 highlighted the city's barely contained class, ethnic, and religious divisions. First came the springtime revolutionary violence of the Paris Commune, which New Yorkers of all classes watched with great interest. The specter of class violence took hold of the city's collective imagination in the wake of the bloodshed in Paris. For the remainder of the decade, the commune's shadow hovered over New York political battles. Exiled communards moved to the city's working-class neighborhoods; some refugees from Paris took leading positions on the radical Committee of Public Safety. Each year, an annual dinner in commemoration of the commune brought together hundreds of European militants.[8]

In turn, conservative New Yorkers viewed any and all evidence of local working-class protest through a French lens, finding a wealth of evidence of the rising threat of communism on this side of the Atlantic. E. L. Godkin, obsessed with news from Paris in 1871, offered two somewhat conflicting readings of the year's violence. The *Nation*'s editor first denounced the commune as an exclusively French event, typifying that nation's tradition of irrational extremism. Yet the international implications of the Continental conflict also caught Godkin's attention:

> But the doings of the Commune, however incomplete they may have been, and however much they may have helped to injure the Socialist cause in the estimation of the world, will undoubtedly help to stimulate the "labor reform movement" for the present in other countries.

Even America was vulnerable, as Godkin worried that long-standing sentiments of patriotism were giving way to "a strong class feeling."[9]

Even as the public was swept up by the events in Paris,

with Manhattan dailies competing for the most reliable coverage of the commune, New Yorkers experienced a dramatic series of shocks at home between April and November. A burst of intra-Irish violence exploded with the Orange Day riots of July, the second eruption of ethnoreligious violence in thirteen months. One year earlier, Irish Protestants had attacked a group of Irish Catholic workers in the Elm Park Riot on Orange Day, July 12, 1870. Exactly one year later, on the most bitterly contested date on the Irish ceremonial calendar, a Protestant parade brazenly marched through the Catholic neighborhoods on Eighth Avenue. In the ensuing riot, sixty-two New Yorkers died; the victims were primarily Irish Catholics, killed when the New York State militia fired wildly on the crowd.[10]

For the rest of Reconstruction, July 1871 was a decisive turning point for all Irish American New Yorkers, Catholic and Protestant alike. The historian Michael A. Gordon has characterized the second of the Orange Riots as the defining moment in the "nativist revival" of the early 1870s. Defenders of the militia framed their accounts of the riots in terms of the rights of Protestants. For the anti-Catholic editors of the *Times*, it was "now decided that Protestants have only such rights as Catholics choose to accord them." The *Tribune* appealed for American-born Protestants to rise up and destroy what was viewed as the "Irish working-class domination of the city." In 1873, the best-selling nativist Joel Tyler Headley, long one of the most bitterly anti-Catholic writers in the city, penned the most widely read history of the Orange Riots. Across the pages of *The Great Riots of New York City, 1712–1873*, the two upheavals of 1871—the Paris Commune and the Manhattan Orange Riots—were linked and viewed as part of a transatlantic threat.[11]

Within weeks of the July violence, local anti-Tammany activists appropriated the memory of the Orange Riots to advance the cause of comprehensive municipal reform. In August, "Civil Rights: A History of the New York Riot of 1871" appeared, featuring a compilation of *Times* and *Tribune* articles on the summer's events. The political cartoonist Thomas Nast contributed illustrations. The pamphlet would turn out to be one of the most influential of the thousands published during the Reconstruction era in New York, for it linked July's ethnic explosion to a larger, still-mobilizing revolt of the city's elite. A subtitle suggested this new connection: "The Hibernian Riot and 'The Insurrection of the Capitalists.'" Denounced on the pamphlet's pages was the "Riot Hibernianic" for "communism, Murder, Socialism, Robbery, Arson."

In the final weeks of the summer of 1871, local anti-Tammany forces—both Republican and Democrat—achieved their most united front of the entire nineteenth century. Even as the Orange Riots raged in July, the *Times* had begun publishing a monthlong series of exposés on the astronomical frauds of the Tweed ring; the numerous stories were collected and reprinted in a special supplement on July 29. Through August, local dailies reported regularly on previously undisclosed areas of municipal corruption. The city's debt, it was reported, had tripled to $90 million in the four years since 1867. Front-page stories publicized Tweed's personal fortune, his funding of parochial schools, and the ring's elaborate system of control in city government. The vast scale of Tweed's corruption—financial, political, and moral—allowed an unlikely coalition of former opponents to unite.

On September 4, 1871, inspired by the revelations and enraged by the year's mob violence at home and abroad, a

Committee of Seventy coalesced as the leading voice of a new generation of municipal reformers. This historic group mounted a political and legal campaign that brought about the defeat of the Tweed political machine and a year later crafted a new municipal charter. Liberty lay at the core of the Committee of Seventy's rhetoric, here defined in negative terms as the freedom of the better classes from corruption and mob rule. In Nast's cartoons and in the ideological tracts of Samuel J. Tilden, these reformers cast Boss Tweed as head of a cabal of dangerous criminals, conspiring to despoil virginal American Liberty.

Born in Germany and raised amid the revolutionary spirit of 1848, Thomas Nast arrived in New York as a child and grew up amid the radical German community of lower Manhattan. Nast was America's leading political cartoonist by the end of the Civil War, and his work appeared in *Harper's Weekly* and other local and national publications throughout Reconstruction. Where his art in the 1860s had emphasized the struggles of the freedpeople in the South, his preferred subject in the early 1870s was the extraordinary fall of the Tweed ring and other political scandals in his home city. To a national audience, Nast portrayed Tweed and his cronies as vultures living on the carcass of urban democracy. Liberty was personified in the form of a native-born, white Protestant woman. Nast's illustrations conveyed a deepening pessimism about democratic culture; municipal corruption in New York City, in Nast's rendering, represented a deep perversion of American values.[12]

A week after the Committee of Seventy first convened, Samuel J. Tilden issued a circular, signaling his break from the city's Democratic Party leadership. This was no small announcement, as Tilden remained chair of the state party.

Tilden railed against centralizing tendencies in government, whether among Republicans in Washington, D.C., or now with some of his fellow Democrats in Tammany Hall. Employing a by-now-familiar rhetorical tool, Tilden explained that he had broken with other Democrats so as to attack "the gangrene of corruption." Tilden was willing to risk a short-term disaster for his party in hopes of its long-term survival. Writing to his fellow Democrat Robert Minturn, Tilden argued that the state party needed to "take our chances of possible defeat now, with resurrection hereafter." For the rest of his public life, Tilden worked according to this prescription.[13]

The November 1871 election was a disaster for Tammany Hall. The reform candidate, William Havermeyer, was swept into Manhattan's mayoral office. The reformers achieved a massive victory: in addition to the mayoralty, they would control all fifteen aldermanic seats, fifteen of twenty-one assistant aldermanic seats, fourteen of twenty assembly seats from Manhattan, and four of five senate seats. The new state assembly would include almost one hundred anti-Tammany members out of a body of one hundred twenty-eight.[14]

Greeley's Last Campaign

The Committee of Seventy's success was significant nationally. Built on a defense of liberty, the rhetoric, ideology, and iconography of the 1871 reform campaign served as model in the next year's presidential campaign. Liberty, defined in negative terms, lay at the heart of the Liberal Republican movement of 1872, with its platform of free-market economics and universal amnesty for ex-Confederates. As espoused by Horace Greeley, the longtime editor and now Liberal Republican standard bearer, this laissez-faire liberalism had lost patience with federal Reconstruction policies, and especially with President Grant's leadership. Greeley and other Liberal Republicans called for an immediate end to the national army's presence in the South. New York City reformers played crucial roles in the formation of this splinter party, a faction that helped set in motion Reconstruction's end five years later. Greeley's presidential campaign gave the Liberal Republican insurgency a distinctly New York character.

Horace Greeley was a strange choice to lead the Liberal Republicans. An outspoken reformer with past connections to transcendentalists, utopian socialists, and women's rights activists, Greeley's nomination as the party's candidate for president alienated many, including E. L. Godkin. After his failure to secure black suffrage at the 1867–1868 state constitutional convention, Greeley had also steadily distanced himself from the leadership of the Republican Party. Looking ahead to 1870, Greeley confided to a friend that he hoped "that the new year before us will bring peace with freedom." This would serve as the ideological core of his national campaign in 1872. On the campaign trail, Greeley delinked black rights from his understanding of liberty; seven years into Reconstruction, the New York reformer abandoned his earlier belief that black freedom was necessary for American freedom. Instead, Greeley used his final campaign to refine a laissez-faire ideology of race for the city and the nation.[15]

American laissez-faire liberalism emerged in large measure amid a backlash against Reconstruction's ambitious project of interracial democracy. Greeley voiced a novel understanding of liberty in a May 1872 speech to Poughkeepsie, New York's African American community. Just weeks before receiving the Liberal Republican nomination, Greeley addressed a benefit for the local A.M.E. Zion Church and charted a new course on the issue of race, one very different from what he had pursued at Albany in 1867. The editor opened by declaring "the colored people are here, and are destined to remain here—our fellow citizens, sympathizing, acting, suffering and rejoicing with us as an integral portion of the American people." This was a typical Liberal Republican opening, proudly proclaiming a tolerant acceptance of the African American right to exist in the United States. Greeley even went on to hint at an expansion of political equality.[16]

Here in Greeley's speech, however, mild support gave way to criticism as he expounded on the theme of "Self-Trust." What followed was a long list of alleged character flaws among New York's black population. Greeley criticized African Americans who "assume that they need more help from outside than they actually need, and they wait for and expect aid from others, where they might in a more heroic spirit, prove sufficient to themselves." Greeley tackled the topic of black dependency with great relish, alleging that African American New Yorkers were "inclined to lean on and expect help from other races, beyond what is reasonable and beyond what is wholesome." For Greeley, demands for governmental assistance were redefined as dependency; as he put the point, "leaning is one of the cardinal vices of our time." Federal aid was thus labeled a self-defeating proposition, leading black citizens into a vicious and unbreakable circle of dependence. Invoking the 1865 promise of forty acres and a mule for emancipated African Americans in order to mock it, Greeley recalled Southern blacks who "stood around for a year or two" waiting for the promised reparations. The Liberal Republican went so far as to suggest fulfillment of that promise would have been worse for black Americans. Before closing, Greeley bragged about his harsh treatment of black beggars on the streets of Manhattan.[17]

In Greeley's 1872 campaign, race was the issue that enabled Liberal Republicans across the nation to define an ideology of liberty that explicitly delegitimized claims made by the powerless on the national government. It didn't take long for other New Yorkers to voice grave misgivings about Greeley's refashioning of reform. Three weeks after the Poughkeepsie speech, a working black New Yorker was one of the first to answer Greeley's novel conception of the relationship between race and liberty. Samuel Wright wrote to Greeley in hopes of landing a position at the *Tribune*. Much of Wright's letter, however, concerned the reaction among New York City's African American men and women to Greeley's widely circulated speech. Wright informed the editor of "a pretty strong feeling [that] is developing itself among colored people as well as white, against" the Liberal Republican ticket. In exchange for employment at the paper, Wright promised to "volunteer to set the colored people right on the Greeley question." In closing, Wright repeated Greeley's claims to being a friend of black New Yorkers before noting that the *Tribune* didn't have "a single colored man in his employ." In short, Wright questioned Greeley's claim that blacks had no further claims on white New Yorkers.[18]

The Greeley campaign began with great hopes but quickly foundered. A July letter to his daughter Gabrielle anticipated a successful fight against President Grant. As Election Day neared, however, the summer's optimism gave way to a growing despair. By October 18, Greeley wrote "my sky is darkened" for his wife was nearing death; she died less than two weeks before voters would go to the polls. As his world fell apart around him, the candidate acknowledged, "I am glad the election will soon be over." Greeley's campaign came to an altogether tragic close in November 1872. On the morning of November 29, less than a month after Grant was reelected by a large majority, Greeley scribbled a "Very Private" letter to his friend Margaret Allen, with instructions to "show this note to no one, and destroy it." Greeley voiced a profound pessimism in the wake of his wife's death and his electoral defeat. He confided, "I am not dead, but wish I were. My house is desolate, my future dark, my heart a stone. I cannot shed tears; they would bring some relief. A bell tears for me, but do not write again till a brighter day, which I fear will never come." Later that day, Greeley died; he was sixty-one.[19]

"The Use of the Streets"

The year 1873 ushered in the worst economic collapse Americans had ever experienced. As President Grant began his second term in Washington, D.C., the nation and its leading city entered a half-decade-long period of economic contraction, mass unemployment, and escalating class tensions. Federal Reconstruction itself would end before the prolonged depression was corrected. The political mood in New York City shifted dramatically, with a rising desperation evident on all sides. New York's radical labor community mounted a vigorous campaign for relief in late 1873 and early 1874, one that ended with New Yorkers fighting over the free use of the city's streets and squares.

A December 11, 1873, mass meeting of New York workers, one of many such assemblies which called for immediate action by local, state, and federal authorities on behalf of the urban poor and unemployed, proclaimed "The Dawn of Liberty." Several speeches made by leaders of the International Workingmen's Association (IWA) demanded public works to ensure the "liberty of workingmen." George H. Hart's address, the evening's last, proclaimed a "Second Declaration of Independence." In his remarks, the radical socialist Hart elevated liberty above life as the most cherished of inalienable rights. As had other New Yorkers in the increasingly harsh years of the early 1870s, radical labor employed a language of liberty to advance their claims for justice from municipal and state authorities.[20]

Weeks later, the redefinition of positive liberty—freedom to work, vote, congregate in public—by many working New Yorkers came into violent conflict with the negative definition of liberty of the city's wealthy classes. On January 6, 1874, the now-Republican Gov. John A. Dix delivered his annual address to the legislature. For months, working New Yorkers had awaited the governor's first words of the new year, hoping for some promise of relief from the hard depression winter of 1873–1874. Dix's words, however, did little to calm their growing unrest. Dix rejected the argument that government had to ameliorate the desperate conditions in the state's cities. Rather, he told the people of New York that "retrenchment in public expenditures" would be his guiding principle.[21]

Faced with the Governor's washing of his hands, Manhattan's unemployed workers redoubled their efforts to secure relief from local and state authorities. A January mass rally of workingmen at Union Square marched on City Hall. Led by the radical Theodore Banks of the IWA, the assembled unemployed workingmen were turned back by a large police force. Delegated to present the aldermen with the group's petition for immediate employment, Banks issued a threat: if the municipal officers didn't provide jobs and food for the city's poor, the working men were prepared "to take it in spite of them."[22]

That evening, one hundred fifty workingmen of the Seventeenth Ward met at Cogan's Hall at First Avenue and Eleventh Street. Many of the men who had marched on City Hall that morning now came together to plan their next collective action. Peter J. McGuire, a twenty-year-old carpenter who would become a leading figure in the Gilded Age labor movement, led the meeting as it agreed upon a series of fundamental demands, including a "rigid enforcement" of the eight-hour laws on both private and public works and an immediate 25 percent rent reduction. The workingmen went so far as to issue a call for a general rent strike by all unemployed New Yorkers until May 1. Further, if no work was forthcoming from the municipal or state governments, the men formed a Committee of Safety that was ordered "to supply themselves and send all the bills to the city treasury to be paid." Finally, the workingmen of the Seventeenth Ward agreed to hold a mass meeting of all the unemployed "irrespective of occupation" in nearby Tompkins Square the following week, on January 13.[23]

Over the next week, dissent arose among working New Yorkers. Several leading metropolitan trade unions came out in opposition to the movement of the unemployed. Led by the Workingmen's Union of the City of New York, the opposition blasted the protesters as "Communists, Internationals, demagogues, and ill-disposed persons." The Iron Molders Union Number 25 was particularly vehement in denouncing the Committee of Safety; the union called for a more moderate labor politics dedicated to the "identity of interests between the employers and employed."[24]

Worried by the escalating class tensions and in hopes of maintaining a tenuous order amid the economic downturn, the municipal authorities attempted to block the proposed Tompkins Square demonstration. As late as the night of

January 12, police told the Committee of Safety that Tompkins Square could not be used. On behalf of the committee, Peter J. McGuire argued that the expected crowd of twenty thousand "had a perfect right to march wherever they chose." After the city police denied the marchers' petitions, the organizers turned to Governor Dix for assistance. The Republican governor immediately telegraphed the following response: "The municipal authorities are authorized to regulate the use of the streets. I cannot interfere." Nor did he care to. Dix enthusiastically supported the city government's decision to place New York's police force on duty for the entire day of January 13. On the matter of suppressing radical working-class protest, Governor Dix and Mayor Havermeyer could agree on a clear program of governmental action.

Finally, late on the night of January 12, the Committee of Safety sought a compromise with the municipal government. The organizers proposed to cancel the march and hold only a peaceful assembly in Tompkins Square. The next day, over sixteen hundred policemen were on patrol in the square and in the surrounding working-class neighborhood. By 9 a.m., a crowd in the hundreds had already assembled. An hour later, the numbers exceeded ten thousand, in anticipation of the promised 11 a.m. start of the mass meeting. At 10:45 a.m., thousands of police entered the square, ordering the crowd to halt. Seven thousand police wielding clubs and nightsticks took control of the square, injuring scores of the protesters.[25]

After the police had violently cleared Tompkins Square, Justus Schwab, carrying a red flag, led a number of the unemployed in a march down Avenue A. The police were quick to arrest Schwab and several of the other marchers. By the end of the day, the police had arrested thirty-five of the protesters. While in prison, many of those arrested were interviewed by the local press and released statements to the public.

Schwab's remarks, published in that evening's *Tribune*, spoke angrily on the workingmen's right to the streets and that the "police had no right to interfere." When asked what right he, a German immigrant, had to protest, Schwab proclaimed that "he was a citizen of the world and recognized no nationalities."[26]

The events in Tompkins Square signaled to many Manhattanites that a new, dangerous phase of urban class politics had arrived. Even New Yorkers opposed to the march deemed the police actions excessive. Whitelaw Reid, Republican editor of the *Tribune*, wondered what "serious harm would have resulted from the gathering if a calmer and more politic course had been adopted," and admitted that "the clubbing began before other means of putting an end to the demonstration had been exhausted."

Soon after the January police riot, the *Sun*'s editor, John Swinton, popularized a radical labor version of the incident in his pamphlet, "The Tompkins Square Outrage." Reflections on the police violence enabled Swinton to enlarge his understanding of liberty. Where earlier in the decade Swinton had advocated a white man's liberty, he now called for a police board elected by universal suffrage, in the belief that control of the police needed to reside squarely in the public realm. Swinton's opposition to the Fourteenth Amendment and Chinese immigration was replaced in 1874 with a demand for "equal rights for all." By no means did Swinton—or the large majority of New York City's white workers—abandon their long-held racism. However, an equal rights understanding of liberty offered Swinton and other New Yorkers a way to contest the bourgeois redefinition of urban politics that remained a persistent danger in the hard times of 1874.

PART THREE

THE ENDS OF RECONSTRUCTION

(1874–1880)

7

TILDEN'S AMERICA

"Reform can only be had by a peaceful Civil Revolution."

—Samuel J. Tilden, 1876[1]

In the face of escalating demands for public works employment and governmental intervention on behalf of the urban poor from working New Yorkers in January 1874, Gov. John Dix could only reply that "retrenchment in public expenditures [is] required."[2] Dix's attempts to create a politics of retrenchment, however, never quite succeeded. It fell to his successor, the Democrat Samuel J. Tilden, to perfect the politics of reform and retrenchment in New York. By 1876, Tilden would appear on the verge of national triumph. His administration had managed to redirect Reconstruction-era debates on issues of fiscal policy and racial politics. In the centennial year, Governor Tilden would work to build on his successes in the Empire State and nationalize his rhetoric of reform, in the process helping to bring federal Reconstruction to a halt.

Manhattanites endured an especially trying winter in early 1874. In the immediate aftermath of the crash of 1873, the metropolis became home to ever-increasing numbers of unemployed men and women. The bloodshed in Tompkins Square in January gradually radicalized significant numbers of the local working class, which confronted a government that not only failed to offer assistance but actively used its police power to prevent protests. All the while, private employers across a range of metropolitan industries threatened further layoffs. In the year's early months, many New York workers came to refine their labor politics, mixing militancy with an intensifying ideological commitment to equal rights. Amid this economic turmoil and ever-widening class division, Samuel J. Tilden perfected his politics of reform.

Tilden's popularity—both in the city and in time across the nation—resulted in large measure from his image as a leading opponent of corrupt urban politics. In New York City, where Tammany Hall had long dominated local government, fraud, misappropriation, and outright theft characterized the city's Democratic Party. William Marcy "Boss" Tweed's leadership in the late 1860s and early 1870s stood as a particularly sad chapter in the long history of American misgovernment. The Tammany political machine, built on the votes of workers, many of them recent immigrants, played the leading part in the degradation of democracy, which men like Tilden aspired to combat. E. L. Godkin, himself an important ally of Governor Tilden, was on target when he entitled his history of municipal government in Gilded Age New York City, "Criminal Politics."[3]

Tilden and Godkin were not alone. In response to rising class conflict and mounting urban corruption, a broad-based movement for reform emerged across the nation. An assortment of Liberal Republicans and conservative Democrats came together to attack what they viewed as the problems of modern mass democracy. For these reformers, the struggle against urban corruption required both the removal of particular corrupt officials and a general attack on the political power of the urban poor. Over the remainder of the nineteenth century, these self-defined "Best Men," active in both local and national politics, occasionally succeeded in narrowing the scope of representative government. For many, reform was now synonymous with limiting democracy.

In Manhattan, such reformers came together in the early 1870s to take on and eventually destroy Boss Tweed's Ring. At the heart of this struggle was the reform network engineered by Samuel J. Tilden in 1871, a network that would shape the city's public life for decades. Groups like the Committee of Seventy, composed of leading lawyers and businessmen, began a decades-long publicity campaign against the abuses, real and imagined, of urban democracy and Tammany Hall. In the pages of the *Nation* and *Harper's Weekly* and in the volumes of the *North American Review* and the *International Review*, a new postbellum generation came to articulate a modern antidemocratic politics. And Samuel J. Tilden was most adept at practicing this new politics of reform to gain elective office.[4]

Samuel J. Tilden was a Wall Street lawyer, urban reformer, New York's governor from 1875 to 1877, and nearly the nineteenth president of the United States. The course of his public life led him through many of the Gilded Age's great movements. Hailed as the "Great Forecloser" in the world of high finance, Tilden made a fortune consolidating small railroads into unprecedentedly large corporations. During his ongoing crusade against Tammany Hall in the 1870s, he earned the title "Great Reformer." After his bitter defeat in the 1876 presidential election, his Republican opponents brought forth yet another nickname: "The Great Defeated."[5]

Typical of the reformers of his generation, Tilden played the part of the reluctant political candidate. In 1874, as Tilden moved closer to the Democratic Party's gubernatorial nomination, he was careful always to claim that he was forced into public service. Looking back from late 1875 (while looking ahead to the 1876 campaign), Tilden recalled to an interviewer that "in 1874, a peculiar condition of things arose. Unexpectedly to me, a desire manifested itself among many persons, as a means of putting the Democratic Party on a reformatory policy and position, to run me for Governor." Tilden's practice of the politics of reform relied heavily on his widely promulgated image as a man above politics.[6]

At the state Democratic convention in 1874, Tilden was nominated to run for governor; the previous generation of party leadership prepared to exit the stage and hand over power to the man who had done so much to rehabilitate the party since the war. Men like Horatio Seymour, Charles O'Conor, and Francis Kernan maintained discipline, holding off the impassioned resistance of Tammany Democrats from Manhattan. Former governor Seymour delivered a particularly stirring speech in support of his longtime ally Tilden, asking the assembled delegates, "Who is the most fit man to do the work which is before us?" For Seymour, and most other leading New York Democrats, the only possible answer was Samuel J. Tilden, the one Democrat who would meet the pressing need at hand, "that of reform, retrenchment, and an honest administration of affairs of our state."[7]

In the fall campaign between Tilden and his former ally, John A. Dix, each man sought to outdo the other in calling for retrenchment so as to claim the mantle of reformer. Retrenchment, meaning the drastic reduction of governmental expenditures, was invoked by both parties between 1874 and 1876 in New York and across the nation; in the process, Reconstruction's tragic fate was sealed. Tilden and Dix shared a sense that a period of austerity was necessary, both in New York and nationally. The historian Eric Foner has written that the 1874 election "inaugurated a new era in national politics, although one of stalemate rather than Democratic ascendancy." In New York, however, the election marked the moment when the state's Democrats were able to capture the language of reform; for the rest of the century, Democratic reformers from Tilden to Grover Cleveland would build on the successful strategies of 1874. In the *Sun*'s editorial on the eve of Election Day, the idiosyncratic editor, John Swinton, went on at length about official corruption, venality, and abuse of power. He focused exclusively, however, on "reckless Republican legislation and corrupt Republican administration." Reform was now an effective rhetorical weapon for all New Yorkers, regardless of partisan affiliation.[8]

Tilden used his 1874 Syracuse state convention address to articulate his vision of reform for the Empire State. The ideas formulated at Syracuse would be repeated endlessly during the last seven weeks of the campaign; in fact, they became the staples of Tilden's public speeches for the remainder of the 1870s. The talk began with a definition of urban political reform as "a peaceful revolution," one that was "going on to a sure consummation." Tilden's optimism in the fall of 1874 was breathtaking; the lawyer-turned-candidate was thrilled by, and certain of the efficacy and validity of, the "ideas of change [that] pervade the political atmosphere."[9]

Tilden consistently linked the cause of conservative reform to his concern for the devastated economy. His campaign rhetoric in 1874 offered grave diagnoses of New York's and America's commercial and industrial health. As Tilden surveyed the nation, all he could see was business in a "dry rot," "incomes . . . shrinking," "workingmen . . . out of employment." For Tilden, the cause of the nation's misery lay in unfair and excessive taxation. As he put it, "amid general decay, taxation puts out new spurts and grows luxuriantly." A promise to reduce sharply and immediately the state's taxes occupied a central place in Tilden's 1874 program. Reform became synonymous with "retrenchment," perhaps the most powerful keyword in Tilden's politics. For the next twenty-four months, Tilden promised listeners first in New York and then across the nation that "frugality will repair the waste of our resources."[10]

Moving beyond his attack on the Empire State's system of taxation, Samuel J. Tilden launched an assault on activist government at the federal level. Nine years into Reconstruction, he was more than ready to condemn any and all Republican policies enacted since the assassination of Abraham Lincoln. President Grant's second term provided Tilden with an easy target. Beginning in 1873, the press exposed a number of scandals; Republican patronage at the New York Custom House was regularly denounced in the Democratic press. The greatest threat to American liberty, Tilden opined, was the administration's corrupt "dominion which it maintains over the reconstructed southern states," which represented "organized pillage on a scale ten fold larger than that of the Tweed Ring." Liberty besieged demanded a national crusade for reform and retrenchment, one that began in New York.[11]

In the fall of 1874, it was not difficult to recognize that candidate Tilden was already viewing 1876 as the moment when conservative reform could be nationalized. On the campaign trail across New York State in 1874, the Democratic nominee warned that Grant would likely run for an unprecedented third term in 1876. Denouncing even the possibility as deleterious to the republic, Tilden demanded that his fellow partisans act to block a third term by immediately putting their own house in order. The Democratic Party, Tilden insisted, "must remove every taint which has touched it in evil times."

As the gubernatorial campaign went on, Tilden at times was forced to address charges that he was a Copperhead during the Civil War. The *Tribune's* Thurlow Weed, Greeley's successor as editor and a particularly persistent critic, regularly reminded his readers of Tilden's wartime transgressions: "to no call of patriotism during the war did Mr. Tilden respond" was a preferred Weed taunt. The *Tribune*, more than any other metropolitan daily, reached a national audience, especially in New England and in the West.[12]

By 1874, such attacks no longer carried the same weight as they had in the early years of Reconstruction. By the mid-seventies, memories of the Civil War were slowly fading, or, more precisely, shifting in the minds of many Americans. Partially eclipsing the charge of Copperheadism, Tilden had proved his mettle as a reformer with his work on the Committee of Seventy. The Democratic candidate had effectively distanced himself from the most discredited elements within his party in the first years of the 1870s. Mayor William F. Havermeyer offered a complicated yet illuminating assessment of Tilden's newfound legitimacy and political viability in 1874: "While he is not very strong with the masses or leaders, the public confidence in his integrity and general ability would make him a formidable competitor." Lacking strength with "the masses or leaders," Tilden was clearly a new type of politician. The conservative Democrat William Allen Butler, an ally of Tilden's from the Committee of Seventy, described why so many had finally come to support his old friend: "There are thousands of voters in this state who are in the same plight with me—who gave their first vote, as I did in 1828, for Van Buren and Adams, and who would be glad, as I should be to see you governor as the representative of sound doctrines." Tilden managed to appeal to both Democrats and disaffected Republicans who sought reform in 1874.[13]

On Election Day, Tilden won by a plurality of over 50,000 votes; in New York City he outpolled the Republican candidate Dix 87,000 to 44,000. One of the governor-elect's first appearances following his victory was a celebration dinner organized by the Young Men's Democratic Club at the famed Manhattan restaurant Delmonico's on the evening of November 19. Tilden used the occasion to address his own interest in fostering a new generation of elite leadership in Manhattan and across America. A year earlier, in his influential pamphlet "The New York City 'Ring,' " Tilden had written of his "desire that the organization of the Democratic party, and of all parties, should be in the hands of a better class of men than of late years have controlled them." Tilden's Delmonico's speech rehearsed his stock complaints about the "consequences in a republican community of the disregard of the duties of citizenship." Here, as in much of Tilden's rhetoric, republicanism was imagined as a bipartisan ideology embracing the elite of the nation in pursuit of the public good. The governor-elect again scolded the metropolitan elite for their continuing apathy, but also offered up some novel ideas on what he termed the "pretty general neglect of these duties" among the "best class of men." The victorious Democrat argued that "official station does not bring with it as much distinction as it did in the early days of the republic. Men have not the incentive of ambition to take part in public affairs." Tilden defined New York City as a republican community under siege, with elite stewardship threatened by "so many industrial enterprises." His own election was offered up as a significant sign of hope that "there is in this society the germ of a better future for our country." Tilden would devote much of his two years in office to the restoration of older, early-nineteenth-century ideas about republican citizenship and elite rule.[14]

On taking office in Albany in January 1875, Tilden immediately set out to put his reforms into practice by thoroughly reducing the scale and scope of state government. The new governor was committed to a laissez-faire understanding of negative liberty, where citizens and enterprises were substantially free from governmental interference. Tilden's vision of a limited government clearly informed his position on the regulation of private businesses with public charters, especially on the question of the state's railroads. In his first year in office, the chamber of commerce of New York City petitioned the governor for "prompt and adequate relief" from the high rates of the railroads. The Manhattan merchant Alexander Stewart wrote to Tilden demanding "the interposition of legislation." In response, Tilden called for a reduction in government oversight of the railroads, since such control "is capable of being perverted to private injury and oppression."

Pointing to state control of canals as an example of failure and corruption, Tilden went on to argue that the free market was the best solution to the railroad industry's problems, "as private companies . . . can serve the public better and more cheaply." Of course, the new governor failed to mention his long history as counsel to the nation's leading railroads, nor did he discuss his continued involvement—financial and professional—in such corporations during his term.[15]

Central to Governor Tilden's reform ideology was the invocation of the *taxpayer*. Throughout Reconstruction, conservative politicians and reformers argued that those who paid the taxes that supported the government were entitled to the greatest voice in affairs of state. In the urban North and the rural South, groups of wealthy citizens assembled in various taxpayers' organizations. These groups typically invoked the founding generation's campaign against taxation without representation. The nation's prosperous classes grew concerned by the rising levels of government debt in the 1870s; in New York City, municipal debt had increased by over 1,000 percent in thirty years, reaching $140 million by 1875. Leaders emerged in both parties who seized the identity of taxpayer and rallied around a politics of drastic retrenchment. At one taxpayers' meeting in Manhattan, "every reference to the cutting down of salaries and the dismissal of superfluous employees was received with enthusiastic cheers."[16]

Few politicians embraced this politics of retrenchment as readily as Samuel J. Tilden. In his first year in office, the governor cut taxes in half while drastically reducing expenditures for pubic works. Even as the economic downturn continued and class antagonisms intensified, Tilden demanded "a period of self-denial." Other Gilded Age reformers celebrated Tilden's austere policies; one observer hailed "the rigorous methods of Governor Tilden." Until the end of the century, Tilden's administration was regularly cited approvingly by Godkin and other conservative intellectuals. In 1876, Tilden could proudly boast of having remitted over half of the state's taxes. And the governor promised that this reversal was permanent. Reconstruction, for Tilden, had been a national period of waste, and he promised that "self-denial will replace what has been wasted."[17]

Gilded Age reformers were not content merely to scale

back the dimensions of state and local government. Instead, fiscal austerity was linked to a growing disenchantment with popular suffrage. The governor's allies had been calling into question the nature of the vote in New York City. A proposed 1872 city charter revision—advocated by the Committee of Seventy—had called for reform in municipal elections, allowing for cumulative voting with each citizen having nine votes for alderman. The voter could give one vote to nine different candidates, or, instead, give all nine votes to one candidate. The hope was that "minority" (meaning elite) representation would be strengthened. Tammany supporters managed to reject this revision by portraying it as unconstitutional. For the remainder of the 1870s, conservative Manhattanites advocated a range of policies to combat universal manhood suffrage.[18]

Even as Radical Republicans fought to expand suffrage to African Americans in the late 1860s, a national movement emerged in support of nonracial suffrage restrictions. As urban America's property-less population increased, many Northern intellectuals grew anxious over the future of American democracy. Charles Francis Adams, Jr., the Massachusetts Republican, suggested the end of any lingering postemancipation dreams by proclaiming "Universal Suffrage can only mean in plain English the government of ignorance and vice." Four years later, Dorman B. Eaton, a leader of the Committee of Seventy, asserted that "no voter has a right to participate in the care of funds to which he does not contribute." As the decade wore on, many grew convinced that the reintroduction of some property qualifications was the only way to counterbalance the growing numbers of the urban poor.[19]

In his first message as governor of New York in January 1875, Samuel J. Tilden promised a revolution in the government of the cities of the Empire State, a revolution that would encompass unprecedented reforms of the state's suffrage provisions. Elected largely on his reputation as an anti-Tammany downstate Democrat, Tilden promised that municipal reform would be the primary goal of his administration.[20] This initiative was one of Tilden's defining actions, the most significant attempt by a Gilded Age conservative to reform urban politics. His plan would eventually propose to do what no other charter reform or legislative tinkering had been able to accomplish: the introduction of property qualifications for urban voters in New York. Interestingly, there was no mention just yet of suffrage restrictions, with the bulk of the address centering around Tilden's obsessions with state and municipal debt and greater official accountability. In a special message issued on May 11, 1875, Tilden called for the appointment of what would eventually be named the Tilden Commission: the Commission to Devise a Plan for the Government of Cities in the State of New York. His message began with a lengthy discussion of article eight, section nine of the New York State Constitution of 1846, which expounded on the provision for the state legislature

> To provide for the organization of cities and incorporated villages, and to restrict their power of taxation, assessment, borrowing money, contracting debts and loaning their credit . . .

Tilden proposed that the "primary object" of the 1846 state constitution, which he held up as embodying all the best qualities of municipal legislation, had been "to protect taxpayers in the municipalities against abuses on the part of local governing officials."

Governor Tilden went on to argue that the previous three decades had witnessed two interrelated developments: the rapid urbanization of the state and the abandonment of the 1846 principle of taxpayer protection. Tilden blasted the decades-long history of legislation that "so far from obeying the injunction of the Constitution, has been in the opposite direction." City taxes were the prime source of economic stagnation, for "they weigh with a constantly increasing severity upon all business and upon all classes. They shrivel up more and more the earnings of labor." In voicing an emerging taxpayer conservatism, one which continues to shape American politics, Tilden recommended the immediate formation of private taxpayer improvement associations in all the cities of New York State.[21]

New Yorkers across the state were surprised by the governor's lack of concrete proposals and general retreat from immediate urban reform. The New York *Sun* captured the mood of many in Manhattan, declaring that "the utmost confusion prevailed." Tilden seemed to be wavering on the very issue upon which his public reputation and future political prospects rested. The state legislature adopted a concurrent resolution providing for a commission of not more than twelve persons "to devise a plan for the government of cities." Yet, Tilden even wavered on the creation of the commission, waiting over six months—until November 29—to appoint its members. The commission would take no action until at least 1876.[22]

Between the May message and the November creation of the commission, many conservative reform organizations lobbied Tilden for action. That year, the New York City Council of Political Reform dedicated itself to restoring elite stewardship of the metropolis. After surveying the rampant corruption in municipal government, the council argued that "the chief cause of political evils . . . is the failure of the classes who have the largest pecuniary stake in the good order of the city, and who also command its moral forces, to meet their individual responsibility in caring for the public welfare." Instead of an educated elite, the city was faced with a leadership class composed of "adventurers, idlers, and criminals, uneducated, and without either moral or patriotic convictions." Calling for municipal reform that would restore moral stewardship to New York City, the council lobbied on behalf of the legislature's proposed commission. Only the prospect of Republican criticism in late 1875 led Tilden to prepare to appoint members. In November, Assemblyman James Daly, a Manhattan Democrat, advised the governor to speed up his appointments. With the Republicans in the legislature preparing to propose a partisan charter in January 1876, Daly argued that the timely creation of a bipartisan commission would take the wind out of their sails. From the very start, Tilden's bipartisan commission could not avoid partisan politics.[23]

At long last, in late November 1875, Tilden selected the eleven men who would serve on his Commission to Devise a Plan for the Government of Cities in the State of New York. Chaired by William Evarts, the commission's members were William Allen Butler, James C. Carter, Edward Cooper, Henry Dimock, E. L. Godkin, Samuel Hand, John Lott, Oswald Ottendorfer, Simon Sterne, and Joshua Van Cott. Drawn from the ranks of urban reformers across the state, these were the men Tilden had worked with during his campaign against the Tweed Ring. Most greeted their appointment with enthusiasm and interest. They represented the range of the New York reform community in 1875, including two editors, a publicist/intellectual, several lawyers, and a New York docks commissioner. The Albany lawyer Hand thanked the governor for the opportunity, reporting himself able to "very cheerfully and readily undertake to do what I can in the matter which I regard as one of vast importance and a good deal of complexity withal."[24]

The Tilden Commission, as the new commission quickly came to be known, met for the first time on December 15, 1875, electing William Evarts president and Simon Sterne secretary. At this initial meeting, Evarts's optimistic faith in achieving substantive reform informed his description of the commission's charge: "The great need [is] for simplicity in our municipal forms of government. They were cumbrous and old-fashioned just like the stage coach. They were out of harmony with an age so fruitful of time and labor-saving invention. Every business in the land was conducted on a more or less improved scale, except that of a municipal government." The Tilden Commission, Evarts announced, would thoroughly modernize municipal governments in the Empire State.

Despite heading the commission that bore the governor's name, Evarts, a staunchly conservative Republican lawyer in Manhattan, who would later serve as secretary of state in the Hayes administration and as a U.S. senator from New York in the 1880s, had a complicated relationship with Tilden. For over a year, the commission investigated the corruptions of urban government in New York State, yet it strategically delayed its report until after Governor Tilden left office in early 1877.[25]

William Evarts, the commission's chair, rivaled the governor as a central player in the swirling political contest that linked New York and the nation so dramatically in 1876 and 1877. Though he had built his career as a corporation lawyer in Manhattan, Evarts had achieved national fame for serving as Andrew Johnson's counsel during the 1868 impeachment proceedings and by defending Henry Ward Beecher in the sensational adultery trial of 1875. In 1877, before being selected Rutherford B. Hayes's secretary of state, Evarts would serve as the Republican Party's counsel on the Electoral Commission to decide the contested outcome of the Hayes-Tilden presidential election.

In the very different paths E. L. Godkin, Simon Sterne, and Oswald Ottendorfer took to the commission is revealed a good deal about the complex origins of the Tilden Commission. Early in 1875, Godkin, the commission's leading intellectual, had removed to Cambridge, Massachusetts, taking up a long-standing offer to teach at Harvard College. And it was the promise of working on the Tilden Commission that lured him back to Manhattan. For Godkin, it was "a kind of work I would like to do, and which perhaps . . . [might] relieve me of the reputation of simpy being a critic." This active engagement in contemporary politics, moreover, "might help the *Nation*." Godkin simultaneously harbored fears about joining the commission. First, he noted that "Tilden is an active and prominent politician." Such political activity, Godkin believed, might "compromise my editorial independence and impartiality." Worried that the other members would be "mere politicians or fellows in search of political capital, or blatherskite intuitionists of the Jefferson school," Godkin confided to his friend Frederick Law Olmsted that his decision to participate would be based on "the composition of the Commission." His concerns sufficiently allayed, he joined.[26]

By late 1875, Godkin's long personal journey from his support for congressional Reconstruction a decade earlier was nearly complete. The *Nation*'s editor, once a champion of the Republican attempt to remake the South, now worked to advance a liberalism that redefined the role of the government in opposition to long-standing democratic beliefs. Forgotten was the cause of freedpeople's rights; in its place was a deepening suspicion of popular government both in theory and in practice.[27]

Where Godkin approached his work as a commissioner with decided ambivalence, Simon Sterne had pleaded for appointment. In midspring 1875, Sterne advised the governor that, "I am an office seeker, or in other words, I want a say in that Commission as a member." Once appointed, Sterne was clearly the most enthusiastic member. In early 1876, he wrote the governor, admitting, "I scarcely know how to thank you. I am more than gratified to receive this appointment of commissioner." A native Philadelphian who had settled in Manhattan since 1860, Sterne had been active with the Personal Representation Society for a decade. Throughout the 1870s, the young lawyer had coordinated a network of reformers devoted to suffrage reform in New York City. Tilden's Commission, to Sterne, seemed the perfect opportunity to advance a long-developing movement.[28]

Oswald Ottendorfer, the reform-minded editor of the German language *Staats Zeitung*, was more representative of the commission's middle ground. Tilden's most important ally in Manhattan's immigrant communities, he was an eminent opponent of municipal corruption. As Tilden moved to Albany in early 1875, the German American editor was rejecting the numerous calls for charter revision, arguing that "such proposals, if they should ever become law, rather tend to create new and worse difficulties." Ottendorfer viewed the repeated charter revisions of the previous decade as a history of failure and advocated something more radical to cure the ills of city government. In February 1875, well before Governor Tilden issued a call for one, the editor demanded the appointment of "a commission of prominent, experienced and able men whose task shall be a revision of our entire municipal Administration and of all law appertaining to it." An unelected commission would be able to reform the very foundations of city government, something politically driven charters had proven unable to accomplish. Ottendorfer celebrated the eventual creation of the Tilden Commission and was pleased to serve thereon.[29]

The commission waited until early 1877 to issue its report. In the interim, however, Governor Tilden grew to rely more and more on unelected commissions—which came to embody all the complexities of Gilded Age reform—to solve seemingly intractable problems. His other widely debated commission was designed to clean up the corruption that had long plagued the canals of the Empire State. Tilden established several other commissions in hopes of enacting his ambitious reform agenda.

In the centennial year of 1876, the governor made history by appointing Josephine Shaw Lowell as a commissioner of the New York State Board of Charities, the first woman appointed to such a high state office. The daughter of prominent Boston abolitionists and the sister of Robert Gould Shaw, the heroic commanding officer of the Massachusetts Fifty-fourth Regiment in the Civil War, Lowell had been active in New York City reform circles since serving on the U.S. Sanitary Commission during the war. From 1873 to 1876, she helped lead the State Charities Aid Association, writing many of the organization's reports on the poor of New York City. By 1876, Lowell had a well-earned reputation as one of the city's leading reformers on the issue of urban poverty.[30]

In her work as state commissioner, Josephine Shaw Lowell demonstrated that there was room within Tilden's reform vision of conservative elite stewardship for women as public servants. Indeed, unelected commissions helped break down traditional gendered ideas about leadership. Lowell was but the first of several New York women in the Gilded Age and the Progressive Era to gain access to public life through appointment to undemocratic commissions.

Lowell was included within Tilden's reform coalition in part because of her numerous writings on "able-bodied paupers." No coddler of the poor, the new state commissioner's ideas on reform had been formed amid her wartime work with the Sanitary Commission and reflected a dedication to rendering charity a scientific enterprise. In the State Board of Charities Annual Report for 1877, Lowell called the legislature's attention to "the heavy expense and great evils resulting . . . from the large numbers of able-bodied vagrants and tramps." Most significantly, Lowell claimed that the vast majority of the "tramps" were young and native-born. Later in 1877, she would issue a special "Report on the Subject of Vagrancy." Recognizing that the system of workhouses that she had long advocated would be insufficient, Lowell demanded immediate and comprehensive reform. Calling for "Reformatories, not prisons," her report stipulated that "time must be allowed for education, moral, mental, and physical."[31]

Lowell's vision complemented Governor Tilden's own reform ideology. The commissioner advocated harsher treatment of paupers and the disfranchisement of able-bodied tramps, all the while asking that poor relief be removed from politics. Lowell argued that "a comparatively small number of persons should be entrusted with the execution of the plan, and they should not be liable to be removed from office capriciously or at short intervals; that is, they should not be elective officers, subject to political influences."[32]

In early September 1876, Governor Tilden attended the meeting of the State Conference on Charities in Saratoga, where Josephine Shaw Lowell delivered her first major public address as commissioner. The meeting was held in conjunction with the annual gathering of the American Social Science Association. The delegates came to Saratoga to celebrate the new fields of social science—"scientific analysis and scientific methods"—as a means to reform. The assembled social scientists typified the intellectual culture of the late-Reconstruction North: Godkin and Sterne were two of the meeting's more influential participants. After hearing Lowell's address, Tilden cautioned against generosity and sympathy for the poor. Instead, the governor and now presidential candidate proclaimed that charity began with "prudence, caution, frugality and the economy of the thorough man of business." New York's governor criticized governmental poor relief for diverting needed resources from the deserving poor: "We must bear in mind that the industrious millions who keep out of the poorhouses and penitentiaries are also entitled to the consideration and the care of the government." As he neared the end of his career in New York politics, Samuel Tilden borrowed from Josephine Shaw Lowell to articulate a national vision of reform that blamed the poor, criticized charity, and would, in time, seek to disfranchise the state's paupers.[33]

The 1876 Campaign

Samuel J. Tilden had been selected the Democratic nominee for president at the St. Louis convention in early July. On July 14, Governor Tilden celebrated his nomination at the United States Hotel in Saratoga. Among the small circle of supporters who joined Tilden for his moment of triumph were William Evarts, E. L. Godkin, and William A. Butler, all members of the Tilden Commission. This was no coincidence, for the governor's record as a reformer who attacked municipal corruption in Manhattan would be central to the public image he presented across the nation throughout the 1876 campaign. In accepting his party's nomination, Tilden looked forward to victory in the fall and the culmination of his decades-long work as a conservative Democrat. Looking ahead to Democratic victory and the end of Reconstruction, the Empire State's governor promised that "the Republic is surely to be renovated." In accepting his party's nomination, Tilden recognized "the strength, the universality, and the efficiency of the demand for administrative reform in all government," and promised to approach the task of reform in "the spirit of consecration in which a soldier enters the battle."[34]

As was only natural, reform and retrenchment were the central ideas and slogans of Samuel J. Tilden's 1876 presidential campaign, in large part a campaign against Reconstruction itself. The party's platform claimed "Reform is necessary" but "Reform can only be had by a peaceful civil revolution." Under the title "Reform!" Tilden's formal letter of acceptance was published as a pamphlet and in newspapers, both in New York City and nationally, in late July. Tilden condemned federal reconstruction on financial, political, and moral grounds. The ongoing economic crisis, he argued, resulted from "excessive government consumption." Tilden went on to remind his copartisans that in 1868 he had argued that "we cannot afford the costly and ruinous policy of the Radical majority in Congress. We cannot afford that policy towards the South." In the summer and fall campaign, Tilden linked his usual rhetoric of retrenchment and reform to an all-out assault on national Reconstruction.[35]

The Democratic nominee approached the 1876 campaign with high hopes. On the stump, Tilden spoke of the pressing need for a restoration of national unity. A Democratic victory, he promised, "means peace, reconciliation and fraternity among all people of every class and race. It means giving fair play to the healing influences of nature in the restoration of our business and industries." As Tilden-style reform gained its widest circulation as a justification for ending Reconstruction, the New York reformer proved ever more popular with many Southern white Democrats. The governor's campaign correspondence included numerous letters from former rebels pledging their support to this "political savior" who promised immediate reform in the former Confederacy. William D. Porter, a prominent South Carolina Democrat, championed Tilden as "the Great Reformer" in a series of articles published in Charleston newspapers during the presidential campaign. Porter advised Palmetto State Democrats that *"Reform* is the issue upon which the next Presidential battle will be fought. *Reform* will be the watchword and battle cry." The South Carolinian went on at some considerable length to catalog the many corruptions of state and local governments in the postwar decade, abuses "so scandalous as to have made the whole country a piteous spectacle in the eyes of the world."[36]

For Porter, reform meant drastically reduced taxes and limited government. The South Carolinian proclaimed Tilden's greatest reform to have been "reduc[ing] the taxes of the State, and thus confer[ring] upon every property holder in the State a personal and homefelt benefit." Concluding with the core of Tilden's appeal to Southern whites, Porter called for a national administration that "respected the rights of local self-government." The local New York language of reform was nationalized in the course of the 1876 campaign as an ideology of home rule, property rights, and white control in the South.[37]

In both regions, post-Reconstruction reform would lead to the issue of suffrage restrictions. For a longtime Democrat like Tilden, whose patriotism was questioned for his near-Copperhead stance during the Civil War, the end of Reconstruction would provide the opportunity to reunite the nation with a reformed Democratic Party in command. While Tilden's visions of an ascendant Democratic Party proved incorrect, a long-term alliance between Democrats from the urban North and copartisans from the now-solid South would have important consequences for the next century of American racial politics.[38]

In the urban North, Tilden cultivated the support of disaffected Republicans. A number of Liberal Republicans from 1872—including Henry Cabot Lodge, Charles Francis Adams, Jr., and Henry Adams—worked for the Democratic candidate in 1876, while the editor E. L. Godkin lost some subscribers and received harsh criticism for his support of Tilden's candidacy. The National Democratic Committee looked forward to Election Day when "many former Republicans will vote with us." In spite of Tilden's well-earned reputation as a pro–Wall Street politician, such American radicals as Henry George and Ignatius Donnelly actively supported his presidential campaign.[39]

Tilden's campaign attempted to appeal to a wide range of reform-minded voters from both parties and from all regions of the country. To bipartisan audiences, the Democratic nominee emphasized that he had gained power through an alliance with Republicans in the name of attacking "the gangrene of corruption," a stance that had cost him a great deal of traditional Democratic support. At the St. Louis convention, the Tammany headquarters unfurled a giant banner proclaiming that "New York, the largest Democratic city in the Union, is uncompromisingly opposed to the nomination of Samuel J. Tilden." Yet other Manhattan Democratic organizations opposed Tammany Hall and appropriated the language of reform in their support of Tilden's candidacy. The James Daly Association of the Thirteenth Assembly District endorsed Tilden as "a true and tried democrat, and earnest reformer, an able statesman, and a worthy citizen." In the national campaign, New York City supporters of Tilden effectively branded the Republican Party as "the degenerated and corrupt party," while depicting Tilden as the epitome of Gilded Age reform.[40]

Horatio Seymour, the Democratic standard bearer from 1868, was perhaps Tilden's most visible supporter, speaking on behalf of the party's nominee across the nation. Seymour seized on the language of reform and particularly taxpayer relief as the key to victory; Tilden's reforms, he recognized, "are not mere theories,—they concern the welfare of every person, of every home, of every business pursuit in our country." Eight years after Seymour's failed crusade for white supremacy, Tilden seemed likely to deliver the White House on the Democratic pledge to end Reconstruction and embark on "this work of retrenchment and reform."[41]

Amid the general support Samuel Tilden enjoyed in Manhattan, a few dissenting voices were raised to question his redefinition of reform. Patrick Ford, editor of the *Irish World*, endorsed the Manhattan industrialist and philanthropist Peter Cooper's campaign and called on the city's Irish workingmen to break free from the Democratic Party. Ford denounced Tilden's record in Albany. Looking to Election Day 1876, Ford gave the earliest hint of a new defense of the rights of citizens and fired the first shot in the battles of 1877. Ford advised his readers to vote against Tilden-style reform and thereby defend their status as citizens: "the vote is a sacred possession. It is all the poor man owns in common with the rich man. It is, indeed, a holy relic! The only one solitary right left him in this Republic." One short year later, New York City voters would return to the polls to cast a final ballot on the relationship between reform and citizenship at the end of the second founding.[42]

8

"THE PROUD NAME OF 'CITIZEN' HAS SUNK"

In the late summer of 1877, the *Irish World* published a letter from Thomas Devyr, a supporter of the year-old Workingmen's Party. Entitled "The Rights of Citizens," this short letter gave voice to a common worry among working New Yorkers at Reconstruction's end. Having witnessed the unprecedented labor unrest of the previous July, Devyr looked ahead to yet another defeat, this time at the ballot box. Devyr warned the city's workers that

> it is a grave and most ominous fact that the public thought is gradually losing sight of the equal dignified position given to all our citizens by the Fathers of the Republic. That the proud name of "Citizen" has sunk, or is fast sinking, into the far less proud name of employee.

In the next two months, tens of thousands of New Yorkers would rally to defend the "proud name of 'Citizen,'" refusing to allow the right to vote to be confined to men who paid sufficient taxes.[1]

The central issue of the local 1877 campaign became suffrage restriction. In March, the bipartisan Tilden Commission issued its report on municipal reform, its most controversial recommendation being an amendment to the New York State constitution to limit certain voting rights across class lines in the state's cities. Weeks later, the Albany legislature would pass the amendment. However, state law required the approval of two consecutive legislatures before an amendment could be submitted to the people for approval. If a different legislature, one more sympathetic to universal manhood suffrage, could be elected, the amendment would never make it to a public vote. Thus, the election of 1877 became a referendum on who was entitled to a voice in governing the nation's leading city.[2]

Before the Tilden Commission would issue its report, however, the nation remained in a state of crisis from Election Day until February 1877. In the first days and weeks after the presidential election, most New York observers believed that Samuel Tilden had been elected the nineteenth president of the United States. Celebrations quickly erupted in Manhattan and among white Southerners. Republicans faced the possibility of losing the White House for the first time since before the Civil War. Three states—South Carolina, Florida, and Louisiana—remained under federal control as 1876 drew to a close. The electoral votes of these states were the heart of the electoral controversy as two separate slates of electors claimed to speak for each state. Tilden and Hayes waited to see which of the Republican or Democratic electors from each of the three Southern states Congress would recognize.

In the months between the election and the inaugural in March 1877, a range of backroom machinations occurred. One week, Tilden seemed the likely winner; days later, the momentum switched to the Hayes camp. A correspondent for the London *Daily Telegraph* articulated a feeling common in Manhattan in the last weeks of 1876, the hope that Tilden's presumed victory was "happily the first substantial indication that the Civil War, which so nearly rent the Union in twain, is henceforward to be regarded as a historical memory [rather] than as a ruling influence in American politics." As 1876 gave way to 1877, it became clear that such optimism was misplaced.[3]

Even more than New Yorkers, Southerners anxiously awaited the outcome. George Taylor, a Confederate veteran in Richmond, congratulated Tilden in mid-November 1876. Rejoicing in the Democrat's apparent success, the Virginian boasted of having "fought and struggled as hard for your election as . . . for the lost cause in rebel service." Proclaiming Tilden the "political savior of our now accursed country," Taylor went on to predict the ruin of the "radical thieves" who sought to install Rutherford B. Hayes in the White House. Taylor signed the letter "your warm Rebel Lover."[4]

The English observer and the Confederate veteran both misread the political landscape. The struggles of the second founding were not yet over. Tilden's program of reform would have to await the new year, as 1877 would witness a series of struggles—both in Washington and on the streets of Manhattan—as heated and as consequential as any other in the era of the Civil War.

As the winter wore on and Tilden's success grew more uncertain, friends began to counsel the now-former-governor on how best to preserve his victory. At a meeting of New York's presidential electors on December 5, 1876, Horatio Seymour led the defense of his old friend Tilden. For Seymour, the results of the November election "filled our minds with such a deep sense of the dignity of American citizenship." However, if Tilden were deprived of the White House, Seymour warned "the pride of citizens [would be] humiliated." In the last days of the centennial year, Seymour linked the struggle for Democratic victory to a patriotic defense of the rights of citizens. The creation of an unelected Electoral Commission threatened "Revolution. Such plots involve anarchy, distress and dishonor."[5]

The most ironic advice of the interregnum came from Charles Francis Adams, Jr., whom Tilden had tentatively appointed secretary of state in November. Seeking to establish a Tilden victory in the Electoral College, Adams wrote Tilden shortly after the New Year a blunt appraisal of their prospects: "My own view is that nothing will satisfactorily settle this question, but an appeal to the ballot. The simple, fundamental, direct, democratic appeal to the one great tribunal." For the better part of a decade, Tilden and Adams had campaigned for a national reform movement in opposition to universal manhood suffrage. Yet in January 1877, both men found themselves rushing to defend the sanctity of the ballot.[6]

Samuel Tilden's political future hung in the balance as 1877 began. The presidential election remained undecided as the cold, hard winter dragged on. While negotiations in Washington intensified, they produced no clear victor. Many of Tilden's most ambitious reforms—including over eighty bills dealing with municipal administration—remained unimplemented as he left the governor's office in January.

While Tilden waited impatiently in his Gramercy Park townhouse to learn the fate of his crusade against corruption in New York and across the nation, his fellow New Yorkers demanded immediate and dramatic government action on other fronts.[7] On Manhattan's streets, the economic crisis of the midseventies continued and in some ways worsened. One young arrival noted that in early 1877 "hard times filled the city with tramps, and there was a great lack of employment."[8] In January and February, groups of local workers made repeated demands on the municipal government for public works employment. Petitions circulated daily and mass meetings of the unemployed were weekly occurrences. An early February meeting of the unemployed called on the city's aldermen "to relieve the horrible hunger and distress" by appropriating "money that will push forward public improvements that are necessary to the public's welfare." Once more, the city's workingmen argued for relief as citizens defending the public's welfare.

As the plight of Manhattan's poor worsened, national politics again took center stage. In late February, the only such Electoral Commission in American history had met and, by a strictly partisan eight-seven vote, decided the contested presidential election in Hayes's favor. The repercussions were felt throughout 1877 and beyond. The previous year's hopes of greater bipartisanship were dashed. Tilden and his many supporters practiced a defiantly angry politics in 1877, often referring to the Electoral Commission's decision as a "political crime."

The machinations in Washington also led to the defection of one of Tilden's most important conservative allies, the New York lawyer and Tilden Commission chair William Evarts. In February 1877, Evarts served as Rutherford B. Hayes's lead counsel before the national Electoral Commission. Abruptly abandoning his long-standing support for Tilden, Evarts became an influential advisor to Hayes. In one speech before the Electoral Commission, Evarts openly applauded the antidemocratic nature of the Electoral College, asserting that electors could vote however they chose, regardless of any popular mandate. Evarts's arguments helped lead to Tilden's defeat, revealing the inescapably partisan nature of late-nineteenth-century commissions.[9]

Unexpectedly, however, Evarts's abandonment of Tilden led the Republican to shed briefly his usual antipopular suffrage stance. For most of his public career, Evarts combined a class contempt (rather common among conservative Manhattan Republicans) with ambivalence about issues of racial justice. In his work with the Electoral Commission, Evarts discovered a temporary idealism and became a vociferous defender of African American suffrage in the South. The Republican lawyer attempted to ensure his candidate's victory by making a series of impassioned defenses of the rights of freedpeople. In one particularly curious pronouncement, the architect of suffrage restriction in the Empire State recognized the altered political landscape after a decade of Reconstruction, warning that a decision for Tilden would render Southern blacks "the victims of your Constitution; for your Constitution gave them the suffrage, and they are to be slaughtered for having the gift found in their hands." This February speech revealed no change of heart on Evarts's part; he continued to campaign for limiting the suffrage in Manhattan all through 1877. Rather, the Republican lawyer demonstrated just how powerful the politics of suffrage reform had become by the end of Reconstruction, in both the metropolis and the nation's capital. Even the staunchly conservative Evarts could not resist employing a propopular suffrage argument in order to guarantee Hayes's victory.[10]

In early March, as Hayes was inaugurated the nineteenth president, Evarts proudly heralded a "New Departure," a "New Politics." Numerous Manhattan conservatives voiced similar enthusiasm for Hayes's victory. John Jacob Astor, Jr., thanked Evarts for saving the city and the nation "from anarchy." Another Republican New Yorker agreed: "The quiet and orderly accession to power of the new Administration is due more to your efforts than to anything else." This "New Departure" led Evarts to the position of secretary of state in the Hayes administration, where the New Yorker emerged as a leading national voice of conservative Republicanism. The move to Washington also signaled Evarts's personal abandonment of bipartisanship. By late March, one of the new secretary of state's closest friends in Manhattan celebrated the fact that "Samuel Jones Tilden appears absolutely forgotten." For the remainder of the year, the Tilden Commission's chair reduced his commitments in New York and focused his energies on national and international politics.[11]

By summer, suffrage would give way in Evarts's mind to an overriding concern with maintaining order. While the Tilden Commission's recommendations were the subject of heated debate back home in New York City, the secretary of state spent much of July 1877 in eastern Pennsylvania attempting to end violent rail and mine strikes. Evarts, however, was no impartial arbitrator. Having built his legal reputation defending manufacturers against the claims of workers, Evarts resided without misgivings as a guest of the mine owners and traveled about the state in the Pennsylvania Railroad President Tom Scott's private car while exploring the labor unrest. Such carpetbagging made explicit the connections between the local political battles in New York and national struggles over class and race. Opposition to popular suffrage in New York City was one part of Evarts's larger anti-democratic political vision, a vision that centered around private corporations, a laissez-faire Republican Party, and the suppression of labor organizations.[12]

The tainted election of Hayes placed the issue of popular

government—and its vulnerability to attack—squarely before the citizens of New York City. An unelected commission had just decided a national election. To many Manhattanites, this constituted an unprecedented attack on the people's sovereignty. For the remainder of 1877, anti–Tilden Commission forces were able to point to this recent example of the grave dangers posed by commissions, thereby bolstering their defense of universal manhood suffrage. The national and the local were, once again, inextricably linked. As February gave way to March and Tilden's hopes of reform were dashed, many New Yorkers expressed concerns for the seemingly fragile nature of their democracy. Oswald Ottendorfer's *Staats Zeitung*, prominent among early critics of the national Electoral Commission, denounced those "who make coup d'etats a profession." Himself a colleague of Evarts's on the Tilden Commission, Ottendorfer issued weekly denunciations of Hayes's "electoral swindle" and worried over the future prospects for popular sovereignty in America. The Tammany Grand Sachem Augustus Schell called on all New Yorkers to "denounce these criminals and their crimes," accusing the Republican Party of a "traitorous" assault on the people's liberty. Nearly all of the city's newspapers—foreign-language and English, Democratic and even some Republican—editorialized against the workings of the national commission.[13]

In early March, the reform Republican *Tribune* highlighted the shifting metropolitan political and journalistic culture when it published a lengthy diatribe by George L. Prentiss entitled "Our National Bane; or, The Dry Rot in American Politics."[14] Prentiss gave voice to many middle-class reformers' loss of faith in democracy in the wake of Reconstruction and the election of 1876. "Our National Bane" suggested that the leading site of democracy's decline was his own hometown, New York City. Prentiss asked his readers whether there had been "anything in the shape of government meaner, more extortionate, less worthy of respect, better fitted to excite mingled shame, contempt, and indignation" than New York's experiment with urban democratic self-rule. The solution, for Prentiss, lay in the restoration of an earlier system of elite "stewardship," wherein the leading classes guided public affairs.

Amid mounting collective concern over the fragile condition of urban and national democracy, New Yorkers grew impatient with the lengthy deliberations of the Tilden Commission. The commission's original charge—"To Devise a Plan for the Better Government for the Cities of the State of New York"—had promised to revolutionize politics in Manhattan, but not a word had been heard from the commission since early 1876. The *Times* first called for the release of the commissioners' report. In January 1877, Henry Raymond, the paper's conservative Republican editor, asked, "What has become of the report of the Municipal Commission? . . ." Raymond predicted "the public will not willingly be cheated out of some substantial reforms for another year." Other metropolitan editors and politicians quickly followed Raymond and demanded swift and decisive action by the Tilden Commission.[15]

On March 6, 1877, after remaining silent through the 1876 presidential campaign and its embittering endgame, the Tilden Commission at last delivered its report to the legislature at Albany. In articulating their vision of reform, the commissioners inserted themselves fully into the realm of metropolitan class politics, directly opposing the public works programs sought by laboring New Yorkers throughout the depression years of the 1870s. They clearly saw themselves as standing above the fray. The commissioners imagined themselves to be speaking to an audience limited to the taxpayers of the state. Governments, the report asserted, were not created for the benefit of all residents in a community or any "other sentimental purposes." Any remnants of the Reconstruction-era belief in a strong national state that could achieve justice and promote equality were gone. Instead, urban governments were

> contrivances to furnish protection to the industrious citizen, to the end that he may be left to pursue his private avocations with the minimum expenditure of time and trouble in attention to public affairs.

Their conclusion was clear: full citizenship should only be available to the industrious and property owning, yet this ideal citizen should not need to act in public life.[16]

The commissioners went even further in redefining the role of government in explicitly antidemocratic terms. The report celebrated the virtues of nonelected commissions in contrast to the flaws of the democratic process, for "deliberate review" was only possible among small groups of leaders. Articulating an emerging Gilded Age language of class politics, the commissioners advocated the leadership of "the best men," men not unlike themselves, since "good men cannot and do not differ" on the central issues of politics. Here, the Tilden Commission most fully articulated its sense of mission, for "good citizens interested in honest municipal government can secure that only by acting together."[17]

This assertive call for unity was striking. Taxpaying New Yorkers needed to come together to act in political ways as a class, self-consciously defining themselves as the "industrious" and the "good." Here, the report reached back to a previous generation for its ideology. The virtue and independence of the classical republican citizen was imagined in class-specific terms—only property-holding men allowed. At the same time, the commission's anachronistic rhetoric emerged from a deep-seated feeling of insecurity. The commissioners lamented the "general failure, especially in the larger cities, to secure the election or appointment of fit and competent officials."[18]

The Tilden Commission sought to empower the taxpayers of the city and in the process restore the stewardship of the fit and the competent. The first of its two principal recommendations called for the creation of boards of finance in each city in New York State, with such boards having complete control over municipal expenditures. It was its second proposal, however, for which the Tilden Commission would become famous. The commissioners demanded that only those taxpayers owning property assessed at over $500 or paying a yearly rent of over $250 be allowed to vote for the new boards of finance. The poor were to be stripped of the suffrage in certain urban elections, for "to admit to a participation in such choice those who make no contribution to the funds to be administered is not in conformity with the principles on which human affairs are conducted." Here was the core of the Tilden Commission's ideology of taxpayer conservatism: the erosion of universal manhood suffrage was mandated in the name of abstract principles of human affairs.[19]

The commissioners recommended that these two proposals be enacted as amendments to the New York State constitution. In order for the suggested suffrage reform to become law, two consecutive legislatures would have to pass the amendments and then the amendments would have to pass a statewide popular referendum. In short, the supporters of the Tilden Commission faced a protracted campaign that began

with the spring 1877 legislative session in Albany. The suffrage issue grabbed the public's attention from April onward.
Various New Yorkers—leading businessmen, liberal intellectuals, machine politicians, Irish and German immigrants, labor radicals—all came forward to articulate their vision for
urban politics at Reconstruction's end.

Two days after the Tilden Commission issued its report, a
severe late-winter storm dumped a foot of snow on Manhattan. For several weeks after March 9, most New Yorkers focused on the resulting deaths and damage. Few imagined that
the proposed amendments to the state constitution stood
much chance of success. The *Times* and the *Tribune*—two of
the city's leading Republican publications—each expressed
support for the plan, but feared a quick defeat in the state legislature. Simon Sterne, perhaps the most ardent proponent of
suffrage restriction among the commissioners, "was not so
sanguine of the Legislature's taking the same view of the
case." Even former-Governor Tilden backed away from the
commission that bore his name, questioning the wisdom of
such drastic measures.[20]

Early debates in Albany reveal the initial skepticism that
greeted the Tilden Commission's Report. State Senator
Woodlin—the amendments' main sponsor—demanded that
his fellow Republicans recognize that "suffrage was not a natural right." One of his key allies in the cause of municipal reform, Republican Senator Jacobs, rose to the floor and argued
that the franchise should be limited only to virtuous citizens.
Jacobs nevertheless proceeded to argue that the proposed
limitations were objectionable, as they would exclude "large
numbers of the most intelligent people of the city, such as
clergymen, school teachers, newspaper employees, and liter-
ary men." Virtue, Jacobs argued, was not so easily classified by
simple calculations of taxes assessed or rents paid.[21]

Quickly, however, initial doubts and skepticism on the part of the Tilden Commission's supporters disappeared. The commissioners had, at least temporarily, solved a fundamental problem for antidemocratic forces in New York City: they had given common cause to the fractured metropolitan elite. Fragmented by political party, by economic interest, and by cultural background, Manhattan's business class had long been divided to a degree unmatched in other American cities. In 1877, however, the articulation of a taxpayers' ideology managed to address a shared interest on the part of many propertied New Yorkers. The commissioners crafted a class unity at once fragile and potent and one that would endure; various forms of taxpayer conservatism would recur through the city's subsequent history.[22]

United in a growing distrust of democracy, the city's reform leadership came together in the early spring. For the rest of the year, Manhattan businessmen rallied around the Tilden Commission and its program of taxpayer conservatism. The New York City Chamber of Commerce placed the commission's proposals at the top of its reform agenda for 1877. Three weeks after the report's release, the chamber attempted to focus public attention on the proposal for suffrage restriction. From the stage at the headquarters of the chamber of commerce, William A. Butler—himself a member of the Tilden Commission—called the "unusually large" meeting to order. The attending members were responding to a special call "to urge appropriate action by the legislature upon the report recently submitted." Describing the Tilden Commission's intention as "to exclude only the irresponsible, floating, and shiftless vote," Butler claimed that the proposed amendments were simply a "common-sense solution" to the problem of urban democracy.[23]

Simon Sterne followed Butler on stage. Sterne began by

repeating the "taunt" he constantly heard about commercial men; that "they would not be in the predicament in which they found themselves if they took more interest in politics." For Sterne, the Tilden Commission had found the perfect solution: suffrage restriction. Sterne was positively ecstatic in anticipating that "merchants will no longer find themselves in contact with the loafer element." By 1877, reformers were willing to include over half of the city's adult male population in "the loafer element." Before ending the meeting, the chamber of commerce unanimously adopted a resolution supporting the amendments to the state constitution proposed by the Tilden Commission and calling for all members to further the cause. Numerous commercial organizations in the city quickly fell in step with the chamber of commerce in support of suffrage restriction, producing Manhattan's most united business class in a generation.[24]

Throughout the spring of 1877, the emboldened taxpayers of New York proceeded to make a case for suffrage restrictions to the larger public. The Municipal Society, meeting at Chickering Hall on April 7, echoed the Tilden Commission's new definition of politics by calling for the municipal government "to be conducted upon business principles." The meeting delegated a Committee of Fifteen to "press the reform measure upon the attention of the Legislature." Among the fifteen were three members of the Tilden Commission: William A. Butler, Oswald Ottendorfer, and Simon Sterne. Sterne, the young reform lawyer, did the Committee of Fifteen's hard work, writing numerous articles, attending conferences, and speaking at political rallies, and in the process became something of a public relations specialist for the anti-suffrage forces.[25]

Sterne radically redefined popular suffrage and gave voice to a new understanding of social class appropriate to the

Gilded Age. His 1877 essay in *The International Review*—written to attract support for the proposed constitutional amendments—began by tracing the history of the vote, claiming that it had long been viewed as "an element of protection." Sterne asserted that in the cities of modern America a new, more sinister type of suffrage was taking hold, with the vote becoming "to quite as large a degree an element of aggression." Sterne imagined popular suffrage as a form of legal thievery, whereby the lower classes could combine "with other ruffians" to elect an alderman and rob the public coffers. For Sterne and other elite New Yorkers, popular democracy threatened society's order, and the vote was but a form of criminal behavior.[26]

Simply put, for Sterne mass suffrage had been a mistake. New York needed to turn the clock back a half century, he argued, and return to an older republican system, the pre-1821 world of property qualifications and elite stewardship. Sterne's preference for this more traditional system of government informed his numerous speeches to the social science associations that had formed after the Civil War. At the annual meeting of the Political Science Association on June 5, 1877, Sterne advised the assembled social scientists that "the adoption of universal suffrage in municipal government had worked incalculable injury." Combining the republican principles of the early nation's elite with the "modern" language of the new social sciences, Sterne arrived at an antimajoritarian theory of politics.[27]

Sterne regularly concluded his addresses by adding the final element of the Tilden Commission's political ideology: the model of the modern business corporation. Again and again, Sterne offered up the same explanation as to why the poor should have no say in city government. Against the chaos of urban politics, Sterne offered up the allegedly ordered world of the corporation, arguing that while "every citizen in New York has an interest in the financial stability of its banks . . . [one] must own stock in the bank before they are permitted to vote." Whenever he used such metaphors of ownership, Sterne was not at all subtle in arguing that the city's administration should follow the model of the private corporation. One had to "own stock" (read: property) before one could gain standing as a full citizen. From the new business world of employers, employees, and stockholders, Sterne was able to fashion a political philosophy of ownership that empowered the taxpayer and disfranchised the masses.[28]

As the spring wore on, the Tilden Commission's supporters grew ever more confident. Meanwhile, debate continued in Albany with most Republicans supporting the proposed constitutional amendments and most Democrats voting against. Both houses postponed their final votes until the last day of the legislative session. Then, on May 25, a warm late spring day, the state legislature passed the proposed amendments. The businessmen of New York City had demonstrated remarkable unity in lobbying for suffrage restrictions. As a result, the next legislature would have to vote once more on the amendments in 1878 and, if they were ratified, the amendments would be submitted to the people of New York State in November 1878. The stage was set for the fall 1877 election campaign to select a new legislature.[29]

While the attack on urban democracy reached its high water mark in the late spring of 1877, New York's labor unions continued to petition the municipal government for jobs on public works projects. Only slowly did the city's workers come to realize that the restrictions on the franchise being pushed by the city's business class threatened their ability to make claims for work. In April and May, as the supporters of the Tilden Commission dominated local debate, few New Yorkers rose up against the proposed amendments; only a rare radical voice could be found to oppose suffrage restriction. The pro–Tilden Commission Municipal Society's April 7 meeting at Chickering Hall was interrupted a number of times by the "communist" Julius Schwab and a few colleagues who booed the first three speakers. Later in the meeting, during the election of a chairman for the assembly, an anonymous radical stood up and shouted, "I nominate Leander W. Thompson as chairman of this meeting; a man that will be disfranchised by you." In a letter to Democratic State Sen. John Morrissey later in April, Thompson himself articulated what was at stake in the debate over the Tilden Commission. The first New York radical to underline the importance of universal manhood suffrage in 1877, Thompson accused the wealthy of attempting "to rob" the poor of "the most sacred right of an American."[30]

The April 23 meeting of the Cosmopolitan Conference was another example of early opposition to the Tilden Commission's proposals. As with the Chickering Hall dissenters, this group was dominated by immigrant radicals who stood apart from the city's central labor movement. George W. Maddox, who would become a leading opponent of suffrage restriction, painted the events of 1877 in stark terms of class conflict: "The crisis is fast approaching. The capitalists themselves are aiding in bringing it about by such measures as the infamous 'disfranchising' amendments drawn up by the Municipal Commission." Thompson's and Maddox's opposition to the commission, adamant as it was, remained uncommon in the first half of 1877. Their particular language of class struggle, acquired over years of involvement with the Marxist International Workingmen's Association, would, however, make its way into the rhetoric of many other New Yorkers.[31]

Anti–Tilden Commission forces slowly mobilized as summer approached; in early June, local longshoremen who worked for the railroads began to strike. By mid-July, a strike wave eclipsing all previous moments of American labor unrest was underway. New Yorkers experienced the tumult with less immediacy than many other Americans. In the city labor unrest was sporadic and limited to certain industries. In fact, New York's largest single strike of 1877—by the Cigar Makers' International Union—did not begin until September.

Events elsewhere in the summer of 1877 did, however, have an important effect on New York's labor movement. During the long hot days of July, the city's workers entered the fight for universal manhood suffrage. Deeply suspicious of electoral politics, most working-class organizations had sat out the early stages of the struggle over the Tilden Commission's report. The 1876 founding statement of the Workingmen's Party was only the most extreme example of this general rejection of politics; it demanded that all workers "abstain from all political movements for the present and turn their backs on the ballot box." The combined impact of the summer strikes and the possible loss of the franchise would lead most workers—and even the Workingmen's Party—to change their minds by November 1877.[32]

While New York was spared the worst of 1877's class violence, the struggles of workers around the nation energized the city's working people. At two mass meetings in late July, the city's labor radicals and mainstream trade union movement voiced a common approach to urban politics and democratic citizenship. The New York Amalgamated Trade and Labor Union held a mass meeting at the Cooper Institute on July 26 to "support the present uprising of labor against the oppression which has not been equaled in the annals of history." The leaders of various metropolitan unions announced their newfound faith in electoral politics. Among the speakers that night was Samuel Gompers, who argued "the workers had a right to strike for their bread and their families." He went on to announce that the Cigar Makers' International Union, Number 144, was committed to a dual strategy of economic and political organization. For the remainder of 1877, the metropolitan labor movement mounted a defense of universal manhood suffrage.[33]

Two days later, on July 28, over twenty thousand New Yorkers gathered in Tompkins Square in support for strikers across the country. Organized by J. W. Maddox, Julius Schwab, and other local radicals, the mass meeting brought together a wide range of anti–Tilden Commission New Yorkers. Having witnessed the state's willingness to exercise its power in settling labor disputes, the metropolitan labor movement's radical flank abruptly changed course and called for mass political action.[34]

The radical New York journalist John Swinton assumed the leading role in the events of July 1877. In his columns and editorials in the *Sun*, Swinton appealed to the city's organized labor movement and to more radical New Yorkers. He chaired the Tompkins Square rally and delivered the night's most important speech. Opening his remarks with his usual dramatic flair, Swinton linked the struggle of July 1877 to the violent fight for equal rights in January 1874: "I speak to you, not less than to the 4,000 rifles that here cover you and the 1,200 clubs now drawn against you!" He called for a peaceful meeting, so as not to give the police reason to use their weapons. However, Swinton was unabashed in calling for militant political action, demanding "nothing short of a political revolution through the ballot box on the part of the working classes."

As the thousands left Tompkins Square, one workingman declared "it was wrong to call this a strike. It is a labor revolution."[35]

In October 1877, as an unusually warm Indian summer drew to a close, one of the most passionately contested campaigns in the history of New York politics commenced. The impending state legislative elections riveted the attention of New York City's workers and businessmen, communists and machine politicians. After four long years of economic depression, and in a year marked by national electoral chaos in the winter and July's unprecedented wave of industrial conflict, New York's politicized citizenry was sharply divided as November neared. And it was the fight over access to the ballot box—the politics of suffrage—that gave definition to the remaking of urban public life at the end of Reconstruction.

E. L. Godkin, the most important advocate for the Tilden Commission's recommendations in the fall, provided a connection between older and emerging movements for municipal reform. In the pages of the *Nation*, Godkin regularly hailed the commission's report as "the most important measure of municipal reform proposed by the present generation." The editor was especially concerned with the seeming threatening rise of the urban masses, in particular the Irish American working class. Opposition to the commission, as Godkin saw it, came primarily from "dangerous Communists and the 'bosses,' " groups that endangered the political life of the nation. A strong current of nativism, albeit a selective nativism, runs through nearly all of Godkin's Gilded Age writings on urban government. Most German immigrants, unless they fell in with the communists, were spared Godkin's ire. Godkin was especially cheered by the presence on the commission of Oswald Ottendorfer, the editor whose paper represented to Godkin a civilized element among recent immigrants. Born in

Ulster to Protestant parents, Godkin looked with growing contempt upon the masses of Irish Catholic immigrants who populated 1870s Manhattan, blaming the poor Irish immigrant for the crimes of the Tammany bosses. Urban democracy was the equivalent of "criminal politics" for Godkin because of the pernicious influence of "uncivilized" Irishmen, whom he described as a race "with hatred for their home government bred in their very bones." Suffrage restriction was required to guard against "the bulk of the poor Irish who drop down into the New York streets . . . find themselves without respectable leaders, and [fall] a ready prey to sharp-witted political adventurers." Godkin's anti-Irish, anti-Catholic politics helped to fuel the Tilden Commission's assault on the rights of the urban poor and to drive a resurgent nativism in the 1870s.[36]

George William Curtis, editor of *Harper's Weekly*, was a particularly reliable and adamant supporter of the Tilden Commission. In celebrating the proposed constitutional amendments, Curtis pointed to only one weakness: namely, that the commission's report hadn't gone far enough. Where the Tilden Commission called for limiting the suffrage only at the local level, *Harper's* asserted that "it should be applied to the [national] government." In a similar spirit, Henry Raymond at the *Times* warned readers that such an opportunity to effect lasting change would "not return for years to come."[37]

In the course of 1877, the one group that was notably silent on the Tilden Commission was Manhattan's African American community. Given that Tammany Hall led the opposition and the state Republican Party largely defended the disfranchisement, this silence was hardly surprising. In addition, in the summer and fall of 1877, New York City's African Americans had more pressing concerns: namely, white "redemption" in the South and the accompanying wave of assaults on black communities. One black Manhattanite recorded his general feelings about race and citizenship as Reconstruction ended. In a letter to the *Times*, "Observer," a New York–born African American who had spent much of the 1870s in freedpeoples' communities in the South, defined himself as a "colored American citizen," in opposition to metropolitan journalists who found the identity "a grim joke." "Citizen" was the most important part of Observer's self-identification. Dismissing "prejudice of color" as relatively unimportant, Observer instead denounced caste as "that which blunts [America's] moral sense, perverts its judgment, and corrupts its manners." Equal citizenship—with universal manhood suffrage—lay at the heart of Observer's war against caste. Nearly a decade after enactment of the Fourteenth and Fifteenth Amendments, such black New Yorkers recognized that the second founding was by no means complete.[38]

On the evening of October 22, the first mass rally of the last stage of the campaign was held at Steinway Hall. Organized by the Municipal Society, several hundred leading metropolitan businessmen gathered in support of the proposed amendments. Several Tilden Commission members spoke, with Simon Sterne contending that "it is almost a solemn duty to deprive that ballot" from the poor. Thunderous applause from the bipartisan audience greeted each call for suffrage restriction as the Steinway Hall congregation tried its best to present a united front. By that October evening, however, the contentious politics of suffrage had escalated too far.[39]

Amid the assembled antidemocratic forces in Steinway Hall, several hundred radicals and workers were seated. Before being removed midway through the meeting, the voices of assorted "communists" interrupted the proceedings repeatedly, heckling speakers, rejecting resolutions, and demanding to be heard "as . . . American citizen[s]." After being removed from the hall, five men were arrested and taken to the Twenty-second Street police station. Crossing Manhattan, a crowd of anti–Tilden Commission protesters grew to over a thousand, boisterously singing the Marseillaise, as New York's radical community mounted its defense of the political rights of citizens.[40]

Five days after the Steinway Hall debacle, a Young Democratic Club rally was held in Gramercy Park, outside the home of Samuel J. Tilden. Four thousand party supporters came out to celebrate the former governor's return from months of travel across the Atlantic. By disappearing to Europe, Tilden had avoided most of the uproar his commission had created, but on October 27 he entered the fray in a most unexpected fashion. Embittered by his presidential defeat and angry over the role played by some of his allies in the Republican Party, Tilden endorsed the slate of Democratic candidates, all sworn opponents of the Tilden Commission. This last-minute political about-face was typical of the unpredictable politics of 1877 New York City.

The last of the grand public meetings sparked by the campaign had little to do with partisan politics. The unionized cigar makers of New York City, Local 144, had been on strike since early September, when the workers at Stachelberg's cigar factory had struck for higher wages. By mid-September, the strike had expanded to include, for the first time, the mostly Bohemian tenement workers. In early October, the *Cigar Makers' Official Journal* reported that "the feeling for better pay has become universal, almost like a revolution. Its boundaries we cannot foretell." By the end of October, the strike was a mass movement, counting ten thousand workers and shutting down at least sixty factories. What is more, it attracted the attention and support of other local and national trade unions.[41]

Members and supporters gathered together at the Great Hall of the Cooper Institute on the evening of October 30. The Cigar Makers' International Union leadership, especially its president Albert Strasser, spent most of the evening discussing organizational business and strike strategy. But that was prelude to the night's most dramatic moment: a speech on working conditions by the fiery union vice president Mary Hausler. A much less emotional speech was delivered by a young union officer, Samuel Gompers. Several times during the meeting, speakers made reference to the current campaign and called for political action in defense of universal manhood suffrage. By late October 1877, labor's class consciousness and a defense of universal manhood suffrage went hand in hand in New York City.[42]

As October ended and the fall campaign neared its climax, the Workingmen's Party was fully engaged in a defense of popular suffrage. Just before Election Day, the radical writer George McNeill signaled the party's complete abandonment of its founding principle of avoiding the electoral realm in an essay entitled "Labor Politics." Here, McNeill connected the defense of the vote to ongoing radical struggles for economic justice, insisting that "the elective franchise is a privilege and power that must be retained by the wage labor class even at the cost of bloody revolution." The experiences of 1877 had taught working New Yorkers the power of the citizens' suffrage. After the national labor unrest of the Great Upheaval, workers in Manhattan and around the country understood the franchise as a necessary precondition for any form of working-class activism.[43]

9

NEW YORK RECONSTRUCTED

The November 1877 election marked the defeat of suffrage restriction in New York. A coalition of the downstate urban poor and the upstate rural poor were able to elect an anti–Tilden Commission legislature. Acting on this popular mandate, the new state legislature rejected the Tilden Commission's proposed property qualifications in the winter of 1878. As the new Assembly and Senate met in January 1878, the *Times* bluntly predicted: "The amendments are in fact as dead as doornails." Even those Republicans who withstood the Democratic landslide in November were scared off the issue of suffrage reform. One observer in Albany reported that Republicans "would not now touch the cause of their troubles with a ten-foot pole. No one is wild enough to suppose that any Democrat . . . would cast his vote for them, and the Working Men's representatives are opposed to them utterly."[1]

It would be simplistic, however, to label the Tilden Commission a failure. Limiting the franchise in New York City was but one aspect of an increasingly assertive taxpayer conservatism in end-of-Reconstruction America. All over the nation, the powerful were making similar arguments in opposition to the "degradation" of democracy. In the South, local white elites reclaimed the statehouses. Across America, Gilded Age intellectual journals, worried about urban life, were filled with denunciations of popular democracy. And in New York, the Tilden Commission effectively moved the political conversation to the right, forcing committed democrats to defend with renewed energy an inclusive vision of urban politics.[2]

The defeat of the Tilden Commission's proposals did nothing to slow the hardening anti-democratic sentiment among New York City's business community. At a meeting of the Taxpayers' Association of the Twentieth and Twenty-second Wards at Continental Hall in early 1878, the assembled members' scorn for the idea of equal democratic citizenship could not have been more pronounced. In one particularly well-received speech, James Gerard was unequivocal in his opposition to democracy, claiming that

> the average popular voter prefers . . . the loud-mouthed demagogue, the man who blows his own trumpet . . . The average community does not like good medicine. It prefer quacks and quackers. The people do not want truth. They do not seek it.

Others joined Gerard in calling for a continued campaign for suffrage restriction even after the election results of November 1877.[3]

Throughout the Gilded Age, many Tilden Commission supporters would look back on 1877 as a noble attempt to combat what they perceived to be the growing excesses of democracy. E. L. Godkin's 1877 pronouncement—that "upon this committee will probably depend the success or failure, for a long time to come, of the most important measures of municipal reform proposed by the present generation"— seemed prophetic to many. Godkin, Simon Sterne, and Theodore Roosevelt convinced their friend the Englishman Lord Bryce of the merits of the Tilden Commission. In *The American Commonwealth*, while noting that the "taxpaying qualification . . . is deemed undemocratic," Bryce labeled the Tilden Commission's report "classical" and called on late–Gilded Age politicians to return to its findings.

Bryce was not merely joining in an academic exercise. Leading Gilded Age reformers continually pointed to the Tilden Commission to support taxpayer conservatism as it evolved in one flank of progressivism. In 1899, the Committee on City Affairs of the New York Reform Club pointed to the commission as a lost, best chance to have attacked the rotten core of American urban politics. The editors of the Committee's *Municipal Affairs* sought to advance the cause of "bettering city government by restricting suffrage to taxpayers." The Tilden Commission, two decades later, "remained the only document upon this subject which we have been able confidently to recommend."[4]

Some leaders of the movement for suffrage reform never recovered from the events of 1877. Samuel J. Tilden withdrew from public life for the remainder of the decade, reappearing only in 1880 at the prospect of another presidential nomination. In hopes of convincing his fellow Democrats that he was entitled to another campaign for the office "stolen" from him, Tilden reiterated his opposition to the "centralism" of the Republicans; again he blasted "the vast power acquired by the Federal Government . . . its patronage, the money it levies, and its various forms of corrupt influence." The New

Yorker defined any contest between the two parties as "a choice between the republic and the empire." Yet, by the spring of 1880, the prospect of a second Tilden candidacy was met with ridicule. Sensing defeat, Tilden reluctantly wrote to the New York delegation to the Democratic National Convention declining any nomination that might be offered. The preeminent figure in the Democratic Party throughout New York City's second founding departed public life: "having borne faithfully my full share of labor and care in the public service, and wearing the marks of its burdens, I desire nothing so much as an honorable discharge."[5]

Even as Tilden faded from the scene, E. L. Godkin maintained his position as a prominent intellectual until century's end. The editor devoted a good deal of time and effort to defending his involvement with the Tilden Commission. As late as 1890, Godkin would announce that "the most serious question which faces the modern world today is the question of great cities under universal suffrage." Growing ever more virulent in his antidemocratic sentiments in the decades after 1877, Godkin came to direct much of his rage toward other reformers who had failed to act in 1877 when victory had seemed within grasp. Not surprisingly, Godkin's relations with fellow members of the Tilden Commission grew strained over time; by 1894, he would label Simon Sterne "terrible."[6]

In the aftermath of the 1877 election, Simon Sterne more than any one individual sought to reenergize the movement for suffrage restriction. In a December 1877 lecture at the Cooper Institute, Sterne's antidemocratic rhetoric was more contentious than ever before; he chose to open with a quote from Montesquieu's *Esprit des Lois*: "Upon the manner of regulating the suffrage depends the destruction or salvation of the State." Sterne proceeded to denounce the election results of 1877, comparing the rule of the majority in Manhattan to the tyranny of Louis XIV. In an urban democracy, the people now ruled absolutely: "The regency has come with us." This state of affairs would wreck American politics, Sterne warned. The people, he feared, "can be flattered and cajoled, wheedled into giving great offices to great rogues." The rambling address went on to criticize the defeat of the supporters of the Tilden Commission while theorizing about the nature of American democracy. Sterne offered a thoroughly Burkean account of the "two sources whence we derive our institutions": the conservative model of the English and the radical ideas of the Parisian enlightenment. For Sterne, all that was good in nineteenth-century America derived from the former. As for the legacy of the French philosophes, Sterne pointed to the New York State constitution of 1846, which had forever removed all property qualifications for white men and opened the Empire State to the influence of immigrants from Ireland and Germany. In short, the growth of democracy in New York was but a steady decline into French despotism.[7]

Having completed his genealogy of American politics, Sterne then attacked universal suffrage more stridently than at any time during the previous year. After claiming that all free individuals should vote, Sterne suggested that only a small minority of New Yorkers could truly be defined as free. Therefore, "persons placed in a position, (as the great majority of women are) which would make their votes simply the echo of the votes of those who are around and about them" should be disfranchised. And this criterion, Sterne asserted, should be applied to all elections—city, state, and national.[8]

Sterne defended himself and his fellow commissioners from numerous critics, admitting that any property qualification would by necessity exclude many good men. The virtuous poor of Manhattan would be asked to endure "a hardship of precisely the same nature, under which exceptionally public spirited women suffer." Predictably, given the decades-long fight in New York over democratic suffrage, Sterne claimed that property qualifications might even serve as "additional incentive" for hard work and thriftiness among the poor. Sensing that the tide of history might be against him, Sterne tried a new rallying cry, suggesting to the audience that " 'No taxation without representation,' should be inverted, and replaced with 'No representation without taxation.' " Before closing, Sterne made one final attempt to reenergize the conservative reform community, proclaiming "our better class voters, in our larger cities, are as much disfranchised in effect . . . as any plantation negro was anterior to 1860." This equation of the urban bourgeois with the enslaved black represented the height of rhetorical extravagance for even the contentious Sterne.[9]

Sterne continued on through the 1880s and beyond, helping to shape progressive New Yorkers' thinking on politics and reform. As one of New York's leading experts on the subject of railroad regulation, Sterne crusaded in Manhattan and in Albany for modernization of the state's transportation laws. Unlike his onetime ally Samuel J. Tilden, Sterne advocated limited regulation of the state's railroads. By the end of the 1870s, he would attack the corporations as constituting an *imperium in imperio*, overshadowing and overwhelming in its character." Sterne's willingness to disfranchise the urban poor didn't mean he viewed America's upper classes benignly. His voluminous writings on the railroads in the post–Tilden Commission years expressed sustained disdain for the robber barons of the Gilded Age: "We must not confound Vanderbilt with Watt, or Jay Gould with Stephenson." Sterne, the commission's great champion of the corporate model of politics, now questioned the virtues of private capital. A year later, Sterne was advocating "public control" of the railroads. Sterne's ideas were nothing if not contradictory in the last two decades of the century. In 1885, Sterne insisted that business and civic leaders were entitled to seats on governmental boards simply on account of their eminent positions. In these years, Sterne turned his attention to the emerging campaign for civil service reform. Sterne was a prominent figure in the Manhattan movement against patronage. By the early 1880s, he no longer viewed universal suffrage as the primary cause of all that was wrong with urban politics. Rather, he blamed "the character of politics as an occupation." For Sterne and many other New York City reformers, civil service reform would replace suffrage restriction as the preferred means of combating the dangers of democracy in New York City.[10]

William A. Butler, another member of the Tilden Commission, likewise pursued other outlets for his anti–popular suffrage beliefs in the years after Reconstruction. Butler admitted in 1879 that while he still remained in favor of disfranchisement, "we are warned off by the whole constabulary of both parties on pain of instant political death. The ark of universal suffrage, in their view, [is] not to be touched, even to steady it." Recognizing the political reality of the situation, Butler still sought "a revival of the spirit of 1871," the high point of anti-Tammany reform. The late seventies, Butler argued, had seen the Manhattan "canaille" once again take hold of city politics; as a result, a new reform agenda was needed. Whereas Sterne joined forces with the civil service reform movement, Butler advanced what he viewed as the next best thing to disfranchisement: an absolute ban on municipal debt. Placing a permanent, constitutional ban on debt was, for Butler in 1879, "the sole effectual remedy for these staggering prostrate municipalities." If suffrage could not be controlled, then the financial power of the city's government had to be reined in.[11]

While Sterne's and Butler's dream of a restricted franchise never came to pass, the expanded uses and powers of un-elected commissions into the twentieth century stand as the best evidence of the Tilden Commission's successes. As the commissioners went in various directions, seeking the next big reform, other New Yorkers turned their attention to the project of exclusion. Local and national politics in the half-decade after 1877 were marked by a series of movements that sought to demonize or exclude specific groups from participation in American democracy: Asian immigrants, communists, tramps, and women. In California, a new political culture emerged, leading to the Chinese Exclusion Act. In New York, politicians such as Horatio Seymour made common cause with their West Coast allies and further nationalized the anti-Asian sentiment of the late seventies, arguing "the presence of the Chinese in the United States is an unmixed evil." Anti-Chinese politics allowed many New Yorkers to refine and advance older rhetoric of white supremacy from the Reconstruction era.[12]

In 1877's wake, many New York intellectuals focused their concerns on the specter of communism in the city. Roswell Dwight Hitchcock, a professor of divinity, declared that "today there is not in our language, nor in any language a more hateful word than Communism . . . it means wages without work, arson, assassination, anarchy." Hitchcock raged at length against radical immigrants from France and Germany, noting that "of strictly indigenous Communism, there is very little among us." Interestingly, the Protestant Hitchcock reserved special praise for the Irish Catholics of Manhattan, expressing surprise that "our Roman Catholic Irish working-men . . . are behaving much better than might have been expected." In the aftermath of the summer of 1877, as radicalism intensified in other metropolitan ethnic communities and a steady stream of immigrants from southern and eastern Europe began to arrive in lower Manhattan, the Irish were steadily viewed as less troublesome, if not whiter, in the eyes of some New York conservatives.[13]

Henry Ammon James, the author of the second study of communism to appear in New York City in 1879, viewed all of the unrest of the preceding decade as a consequence of the foreign (and especially German) ideology of communism. James offered an original argument about the explosive labor unrest of 1877, suggesting that the strikes and threat of suffrage reform had brought workers "into the political arena." Critically important for James was the Workingmen's Party's shift from its earlier disavowal of politics; all of a sudden, "the disturbances of . . . summer awakened in the proletariat . . . an overwhelming sense of its own strength." Anxious in the face of emerging labor parties in urban America, James and others agreed that action was needed to limit the political influence of such "communistic" tendencies.

While certain communities within the metropolitan working class were being branded communist, a new term, the *tramp*, was coined at the end of Reconstruction to designate the transient poor. The word entered the American vocabulary amid the economic crises of the 1870s to categorize the growing numbers of able-bodied, native-born poor. After 1877, as the State Board of Charities widened the field of its exploration of the impoverished and floating population in New York City, a number of reformers organized to disfranchise the state's tramps.[14]

New York women's demands for the full rights of citizenship revealed the limits of coalition-building after Reconstruction. Beginning in 1878, after several years of decreased activism in the state, women's suffrage activists organized a statewide campaign, hoping to capitalize on the recent success of working-class men and further expand the dimensions of democratic citizenship. The 1877 defense of the vote as a "sacred right" was converted by Empire State women in 1878 into an argument for ending the gendered identity of citizen. Where a seemingly universal logic underlay the earlier opposition to the Tilden Commission's proposals, most Gilded Age New York men were willing to reckon with the contradictions of their vision of democratic citizenship. When women demanded the same protections afforded to all men, little support could be found. At the 1878 annual meeting of the New York State Woman Suffrage Association, the group's leadership unexpectedly called upon the memory of the defeated Tilden Commission. The convention claimed that

> each year the necessity for the direct representation of women becomes more apparent in our legislation as indicated by . . . the report of [the Tilden Commission] that only taxpayers should have the right to vote for members of the boards of finance, yet entirely ignored the claims of women taxpayers to the same privilege.

The women's suffrage activists questioned the commission, not for having sought to limit the suffrage but rather for having limited the identity of taxpayer to the men of New York. Matilda Joslyn Gage, the association's president, articulated a new, post–Tilden Commission approach to women's rights. Having defined the right to vote as originating in the founders' fight against taxation without representation, Gage pointed out that "the largest taxpayer on Manhattan Island is a woman." Gage demanded immediate enfranchisement for the thousands of New York City women who paid direct taxes.[15]

Amid the clamor and debate over suffrage's extension or exclusion, two journalists continued the fight for a more democratic New York City. In the decades after 1877, the veteran labor journalist John Swinton and the newly arrived African American editor T. Thomas Fortune fought for a more inclusive public life in Manhattan. Even as Gilded Age conservatism turned away from the legacies of the struggles for citizenship and suffrage, men like Swinton and Fortune kept faith with the best elements of New York's second founding.

Arriving in Manhattan as a twenty-four-year-old in 1880, T. Thomas Fortune had grown up in Florida before moving northward to Washington, D.C. The son of a prominent African American politician in Reconstruction-era Florida, Fortune had served as a page in the state senate in Tallahassee. Enrolling at Howard University in 1874, Fortune began work as a printer's apprentice at the *People's Advocate* in the nation's capital. Upon arrival in Manhattan, Fortune soon began editing the New York *Rumor*; one year later, in 1881, Fortune changed the paper's name to the *Globe*. In the following years, two more name changes would ensue, to the *Freeman* in 1884, and finally to the *Age*. The New York *Age* would remain in continuous publication until after the Second World War. From his base in Manhattan, Fortune edited the most important black newspaper of the late nineteenth century. Not since the era of Russwurm and Cornish's *Freedom's Journal* had Manhattan been home to the central organ of national African American life. Over the last decades of the century,

Fortune rose in prominence to rank as one of Gilded Age America's leading black public intellectuals. He led the 1890 founding of the National Afro-American League, an important forerunner of the NAACP. In the mid-1880s, the *Globe* had a circulation of over six thousand for its weekly four-page edition and a full-time staff of four.[16]

In New York City, Fortune was one of a new generation of voices articulating a democratic and race-conscious vision of post-Reconstruction politics. One of his earliest crusades was against the ongoing segregation of the city's public schools; Fortune pointed to national and state civil rights legislation in a prolonged and ultimately failed attempt to integrate the schools in Manhattan. An active supporter of the 1883 Blair Bill and its promise of federal aid to African American schools, Fortune urged the federalization of public education. The next two years brought the publication of his two most important works, *Black and White* (1884) and *The Negro in Politics* (1885). These writings sought to link the project of black self-help in the urban North to the continued need for federal assistance and protection for African Americans in the South.

Further, Fortune was one of the first black New Yorkers who urged black political independence from the Republican Party. All the while, he was emphasizing the persistent challenge of caste in Manhattan life and borrowing from the works of Henry George to construct an economic theory and a political ideology that linked the plight of the rural Southern farmer to that of New York's working people. In these years, Fortune established close ties with John Swinton, who referred to Fortune as "our brilliant contemporary." The two editors worked to popularize Henry George's ideas and to prepare the way for the next great moment of democratic possibility in New York's long history: the 1886 campaign for mayor, wherein Henry George lost the race but energized new constituencies and built on the struggles of the 1860s and 1870s.[17]

Faced with ascendant conservatism in the wake of Reconstruction, the activist journalist John Swinton used his newspaper work to continue the fight for a more democratic New York City. For the rest of the century, Swinton and other local labor activists viewed the fight over the Tilden Commission as a struggle of great significance. Two decades later, amid the next great wave of labor struggles in 1893–1894, Swinton pointed back to the 1877 New York City battle over suffrage restriction as a formative event in the history of the American working class. Swinton argued that in the struggle over the Tilden Commission

> several things were gained, the loss of which would have been incalculably dangerous to labor. If, for example, the disfranchisement scheme of Simon Stern [sic] had not been thwarted when he was sure of its adoption, or if labor had not brought about its defeat, a good many of the workingmen of New York who still possess the right of voting would now be deprived of it . . .

The most important lesson of 1877 was that coalition politics —or, as Swinton put it, "a more or less satisfactory 'union of forces' "—enabled "good ends" to be achieved and "bad projects thwarted."[18]

In the immediate aftermath of 1877, however, Swinton struggled to achieve just such a union of forces. The editor was greatly influenced in these years by friendships with Henry George and Karl Marx. In the summer of 1880, Swinton had traveled about Great Britain and France, preparing a book comparing Gladstone's administration with the Third Republic. The New Yorker concluded his trip with a visit to Marx at the seaside vacation village of Ramsgate. Swinton had long been in awe of Marx; now he compared him to Socrates and sensed that "his hand is at work preparing the way for the new advent." What most moved Swinton, however, were his final moments with Marx. Just as he was taking leave to catch his train back to London, Swinton asked a wildly philosophical question. The New York radical was unabashedly rhapsodic in describing the response:

> And it seemed as though his mind were inverted for a moment while he looked upon the roaring sea in front and the restless multitude upon the beach. *"What is?"* I had inquired, to which, in deep and solemn tone, he replied: *"Struggle!"* At first it seemed as though I had heard the echo of despair; but, peradventure, it was the law of life.

On returning to Manhattan, Swinton completed his account of contemporary affairs in Europe, placing Marx's call for struggle at the conclusion of his analysis. The book's final words, written in late 1880, summed up Swinton's sense of the lessons learned during the long second founding: "Here we must toil, waiting for the things that are to be."[19]

EPILOGUE

GRANT'S TOMB

New York has never been a city to dwell on its past.[1] Here and there around Manhattan, one comes across a few unlikely memorials to the second founding. On the Manhattan side of the Brooklyn Bridge, a statue of Horace Greeley at City Hall serves as a reliable landmark for tour groups and friends in need of a place to meet. Josephine Shaw Lowell's memorial atop an elegant fountain in Bryant Park stares off toward the seedy grandeur of the Port Authority Bus Terminal. At Grand Army Plaza, facing the stately Plaza hotel and announcing an imperial metropolis and nation for the twentieth and now twenty-first centuries, Augustus Saint-Gaudens's *William Tecumseh Sherman* presides in all its gilded glory. The Sherman monument's easy triumphalism has secured it a position at the center of respectable Manhattan society for a full century. Much more elusive are memorials or even a trace of public commemoration of the 1863 draft riots. Civil War public history, Manhattan-style, seems a rather uncomplicated experience.

And yet, high above the Hudson River at 122nd Street,

awkwardly alongside Manhattan's neighborhoods, Grant's Tomb looks southward over the city, forever reminding New Yorkers of a nineteenth-century past at once distant and oddly familiar. The tomb is perhaps the most famous of the city's memorials, but it is primarily known as a vaguely remembered one-liner from our grandparents' generation. At the dawn of the twentieth century, Grant's Tomb stood as a central site of Civil War commemoration, for national as well as New York audiences. Today, such centrality has long faded for the displaced memorial. The tomb's enduring majesty as well as its uncomfortable relationship with the surrounding cityscape speaks emphatically to New Yorkers' ongoing inability to think straight about the city's past.

Dedicated to the military architect of emancipation, adjacent today to the city's Ivy League university and a number of tenements and public housing projects, Grant's Tomb remains located along the city's enduring racial fault line. We can uncover some of the legacies of Reconstruction in New York by studying Grant the New Yorker, both in life and in death.

In 1879, Ulysses S. Grant returned to the United States. Since leaving the White House two years earlier, the eighteenth president had traveled around the world with his wife, Julia. In the capital cities of Europe and Asia, Grant had been celebrated as one of the heroic figures of the modern age. All over the globe, leading statesmen sang the praises of Grant's generalship in the Civil War and lauded his presidency. Returning to North America, Grant continued traveling through 1880 and into 1881, settling but briefly in Galena, Illinois, to see if he would be the Republican presidential nominee for an unprecedented third term.[2]

In the early 1880s, Grant gave up on politics and set his sights on the financial world of lower Manhattan. Bidding to make their fortune, the Grants settled into a brownstone at 3 East 66th Street, just off Fifth Avenue. The Grants' son, Buck, who cofounded the brokerage house of Grant & Ward with Fernando Ward, lured his father into a series of increasingly risky investments.[3] In 1884, as Grant & Ward collapsed, the former president went bankrupt; among his many debts, Grant owed $150,000 to William Vanderbilt. The personification of Northern military supremacy now became a subject of pity for the Gilded Age middle class.

From the outset, there had been both an inevitability and a desperation about Grant's move to New York City. The Gilded Age metropolis held out the possibility of great riches and dangerous risks for Grant. Those successors who have followed Grant's lead and settled in the New York City area— Herbert Hoover, Richard Nixon, Bill Clinton—have all attempted to live down some scandal or personal shame by embedding themselves in the metropolis. New York City brought new humiliation to Grant but would in time embrace the former president as a native son.

Drowning in debt, between 1884 and 1885 Grant worked tirelessly to complete his *Personal Memoirs*, to this day the most acclaimed work of its genre. Grant's friend Samuel Clemens assisted in securing lucrative publishing contracts, for serialization in *Century Magazine* and for publication as a book. As he worked toward completing his memoirs, initially on East 66th Street and then upstate at Mount McGregor, Grant learned that he had throat cancer. His final months were spent completing the *Personal Memoirs*, which turned out to be a spectacular financial success after his death, securing prosperity for his heirs.

Grant died on July 23, 1885, at Mount McGregor, his re-

treat just north of Saratoga Springs. Immediately, New Yorkers set about claiming Grant as one of their own. The *Times*'s
front-page story the next morning opened with Grant's pur-
ported account of why he should be buried in his adopted
Manhattan: "because the people of that city befriended me in
my need."[4] Such grieving-as-appropriation was part of a *Times*-
led media campaign to have the former president buried in
Manhattan. Speaking to the city's sense of itself two decades
after the Civil War, the editors pronounced that propriety demanded Grant's burial "here, in the Nation's real capital." Before the week was through, the paper cited scores of city
officials and notables, all clamoring for the general's burial to
be in the city. William Maxwell Evarts, now U.S. senator from
New York, lobbied the Grant family in support of a Manhattan burial. Rejecting claims that the family preferred a site in
the nation's capital, one minor official made it clear that "this
is the metropolis of the country, and it seems to me that it is
the fittest place to inter the country's greatest hero."

Even as leaders strategized over how to secure a permanent resting place for Grant in New York, the city experienced a period of mourning that evoked memories of
Lincoln's funeral procession two decades earlier. For three
days, Grant's body lay in state at City Hall. On August 8, a
six-mile funeral procession made its way past hundreds of
thousands of spectators, from Chambers Street in Lower
Manhattan up to a temporary tomb on Riverside Drive on the
far Upper West Side. The historian David Blight points to the
New York procession as an early incarnation of an emerging
culture of reconciliation between white Northerners and
Southerners. In the process, many whites abandoned the
African American fight for racial justice. Grover Cleveland,
former governor and now the first Democratic president since

before the Civil War, selected two ex-Confederate generals to serve among Grant's twelve pallbearers.[5]

The struggle over Grant's memory, and more broadly New York's public memory of the second founding, quickly focused on the work of the Grant Monument Association. Organized in the late summer of 1885, the committee was dominated by the leading figures of Gilded Age New York: former President Chester Arthur, former Secretary of State Hamilton Fish, J. P. Morgan, and Cornelius Vanderbilt, among many others. Over the next decade, nearly one hundred thousand donors helped to raise six hundred thousand dollars for the permanent tomb. At the association's first meeting in July 1885, the African American professor Richard T. Greener was appointed secretary.[6]

A generation earlier, black New Yorkers like Henry Highland Garnet had headed southward to Washington and beyond to engage in the initial work of Reconstruction. In the 1880s, a reverse northward migration began to accelerate, with a new generation of African Americans—men like Greener and T. Thomas Fortune—settling in New York City and taking up the Northern front of the black freedom struggle. Born in 1844 in Philadelphia, Richard Theodore Greener earned honors in 1870 as the first black graduate of Harvard College. Between 1873 and 1877, Greener served as professor of moral and mental philosophy, among other subjects, at the interracial University of South Carolina. Reconstruction's end in 1877 brought about the closure of the school as local whites set out to create an all-white college. Greener relocated to Washington, D.C., where, in 1879, he became dean of Howard University Law School.[7]

Hired in 1885 for the two-hundred-dollars-a-month position as secretary of the Grant Monument Association, Greener quickly became an omnipresent figure in Gilded Age Manhattan. Whether socializing with other metropolitan Harvard alumni or marching arm and arm with Fortune in the Saint Patrick's Day Parade, Greener challenged the city's long-standing racial etiquette.[8] Throughout the 1880s and 1890s, the construction of Grant's Tomb was a profoundly political project, largely owing to Greener's identity as a black Republican. By 1887, Greener managed to expand his presence in city politics, taking a seat on the Municipal Civil Service Examining Board. But the Grant Monument Association remained his crusade. From his office on Lower Broadway, Greener worked tirelessly to raise funds for construction. Eventually a coalition of Democrats in City Hall and Washington, D.C., removed Greener from his position as secretary in early 1892, though he would remain active with the association's work until his death.

Greener's removal took place against a backdrop of mounting congressional criticism of the slow pace of fund-raising and design in New York. In the late 1880s, many American art critics had engaged in a prolonged debate over possible designs for the Grant Memorial, filling the pages of journals such as the *North American Review* and *American Architect*. The editors of the *Century* anticipated that the eventual memorial "will be everywhere known and will be everywhere accepted as the great typical example of American art." Such high hopes were common but little progress took place until the end of the decade. National resentments came to the surface in 1890 as the Manhattan-dominated Grant Monument Association still had not come up with an approved plan for the site. That year, Republican Sen. Preston B. Plumb of Kansas introduced a bill demanding the removal of the deceased president's remains to Arlington Cemetery; Plumb's bill passed the Senate and was introduced into the House of Rep-

resentatives. In the House, New York City congressmen—
including several Democrats—defended the association. In
the final House vote, Plumb's bill was defeated. In one of the
crowning ironies of the second founding, Manhattan Democrats, whom Grant had long struggled against with John I.
Davenport in the 1870s, now led the movement to bury Grant
in their city.[9]

That same year, the association finally selected architect
John Duncan's design. Recently awarded the commission for
the Soldiers' and Sailors' Memorial Arch in Brooklyn's Grand
Army Plaza, Duncan constructed a Civil War memorial rooted
in the heroic architecture of the classical world. Duncan provided an emerging imperial America with built forms that reflected not so much on the nineteenth-century past as they
looked ahead to an ascendant nation in the next century. As
Duncan's design was completed and construction began, Columbia University committed to moving to 116th Street and
Broadway by 1897. The Morningside Heights neighborhood,
as imagined by civic boosters and real estate investors, would
stand as an American Acropolis.

After twelve years of planning and politicking, Grant's
Tomb opened on April 27, 1897, the seventy-fifth anniversary
of Grant's birth. Facing south from its perch at Riverside
Drive and West 122nd Street, the Tomb proclaimed the general's epitaph, "Let Us Have Peace." Over one million New
Yorkers attended the dedication. For the next twenty years,
the tomb was the most popular tourist attraction in New York,
regularly serving as the setting for major civic celebrations.
In the first decade of the twentieth century, with Manhattanite Theodore Roosevelt in the White House, Grant's
Tomb symbolized New York's now-central position in the nation's politics.

For over a century, the tomb has held a powerful appeal to

some New Yorkers. Henry James, on one of his rare visits from England, celebrated the tomb as an exception to the soul-deadening modernity that had taken hold of his native Manhattan. Grant's Tomb, for James in 1903, was "a great democratic demonstration caught in the fact, unguarded and unenclosed . . . as open as an hotel or a railway station to any coming and going."[10] Amid his ruminations on the demoralized culture of New York City at the dawn of the twentieth century, James found himself heartened by his visit to Riverside and 122nd. In syntax and cheeriness atypical of the novelist, James confessed "on the whole, I distinctly 'liked' it."

Since James's appreciation, the tomb has had a troubled history. In 1939, the Federal Writers' Project's *New York City Guide* noted, "it is said that few New Yorkers have ever visited the tomb, and no visitor has ever missed it."[11] In the years after the First World War, the tomb entered into a decades-long era of decline. Only a few decades after its dedication, vandalism already became more and more common. By the 1920s, local students used the memorial's marble walls as a preferred arena for games of handball.[12] Such vandalism and neglect would only worsen over time. Yet, by the last years of the twentieth century, Grant's Tomb stood as a vibrant public site for uptown residents, hosting a range of performances each summer.

One spring day in the early twenty-first century, as the Manhattan School of Music's new twenty-story tower went up at 123rd Street and Broadway, a modern democratic vista was obscured. For over a century, from most spots in Harlem, one could look west, up Morningside Heights to Grant's Tomb. One neighborhood resident lamented that "the monument can no longer be seen from most of the east side of Broadway in the immediate vicinity."[13] The view from the neighboring housing projects is now dominated by the new building, with the tomb blocked from view. The towering new academic structure presents its service entrance to its Broadway neighborhood; the West Harlem sidewalk is often littered with the school's trash.

Grant's Tomb's marble has represented many things for New Yorkers as varied as Richard T. Greener and Henry James. Not the least of the tomb's messages has been a reminder of a liberating army and its victorious commander. To be sure, Grant's Tomb has long suggested complex meanings to those New Yorkers who paid attention: the broken promise of emancipation, a North that failed to live up to the first Reconstruction's promise, side by side with an enduring sense of the city's unrealized possibilities. One more view to Reconstruction past has been closed off, again blocking New Yorkers' ability to imagine reconstruction to come.

NOTES

BIBLIOGRAPHY

ACKNOWLEDGMENTS

INDEX

NOTES

Preface

1. W.E.B. Du Bois, *Black Reconstruction in America, 1860–1880* (New York, 1935), 708.

2. Richard Franklin Bensel has argued that "the Civil War, even more than the end of British colonial rule, represents the true foundational moment in American political development." Bensel, *Yankee Leviathan: The Origins of Central State Authority in America, 1859–1877* (New York, 1990), 10. More recently, Akhil Amar Reed has advanced the claim that in the legal realm "much of our modern Constitution comes not from the creators but from the Reconstructors." Akhil Amar Reed, *The Bill of Rights: Creation and Reconstruction* (New Haven, 1998), 304.

3. Du Bois, *Black Reconstruction in America, 1860–1880*, 708.

4. Sven Beckert has persuasively argued that local industrialists forged a strong class identity as a bourgeoisie during the Reconstruction years. Sven Beckert, *The Monied Metropolis: New York City and the Consolidation of the American Bourgeoisie, 1850–1896* (New York, 2001).

5. For innovative studies that take into account Reconstruction's transatlantic scope, see Philip Katz, *From Appomattox to Montmartre: Americans and the Paris Commune* (Cambridge, Mass., 1998), and Timothy Messer-Kruse, *The Yankee International: Marxism and the American Reform Tradition, 1848–1876* (Chapel Hill, 1998).

1: After the Riots

1. *The New York Times*, July 16, 1863.
2. *Report of the Merchants' Committee*, 7, cited in Du Bois, *Black Reconstruction in America, 1860–1880*, 103.
3. Mayor Opdyke Proclamation, July 17, 1863, Municipal Archives.
4. Iver Bernstein, *The New York City Draft Riots: Their Significance for American Society and Politics in the Age of the Civil War* (New York, 1990), 5.
5. New York *Times*, July 17, 1863.
6. Adrian Cook, *Armies of the Street*, 165.
7. *Diary of George Templeton Strong*, July 1863, quoted in Edwin G. Burrows and Mike Wallace, *Gotham: A History of New York City to 1898* (New York, 1999), 895.
8. "Several Ringleaders Caught," New York *Times*, July 17, 1863, 1.
9. "The Late Riot," New York *Times*, July 19, 1863, 8.
10. "Park Vagabonds," New York *Times*, July 19, 1863, 8.
11. Burrows and Wallace, *Gotham*, 897.
12. *Harper's Weekly*, August 22, 1863.
13. *Harper's Weekly*, August 8, 1863, 498.
14. "Effect of the Late Riots . . . ," *Harper's Weekly*, August 8, 1863.
15. David Donald, *Lincoln* (New York, 1995), 448.
16. Ernest A. McKay, *The Civil War in New York City* (Syracuse, N.Y., 1990), 207.
17. *Christian Recorder*, August 1, 1863.
18. *Christian Recorder*, January 9, 1864, and June 11, 1864.
19. Melville, "The House-top. A Night Piece. July, 1863," in Cook, *The Armies of the Night*, 156.
20. Burrows and Wallace, *Gotham*, 897.
21. Ibid.

2: Black Founders

1. James McCune Smith, *A Memorial Discourse by Henry Highland Garnet* (Philadelphia, 1865) is the source for this and the following paragraphs.
2. Earl Ofari, *Let Your Motto Be Resistance: The Life and Thought of Henry Highland Garnet* (Boston, 1972). "The Gospel of Humanity at Washington," *Freedman's Journal*, April 1865.
3. Philip S. Foner and George E. Walker, eds., *Proceedings of the Black National and State Conventions, 1865–1900, Volume I* (Philadelphia, 1986).

4. David N. Gellman and David Quigley, *Jim Crow New York: A Documentary History of Race and Citizenship, 1777–1877* (New York, 2003).

5. *Proceedings of the National Convention of Colored Men, Held in Syracuse, New York, October 4–7, 1864* (Boston, 1864), 12, 20.

6. New York *Daily News*, January 14, 1865. "The Colored Folks of New York: A Colored Man's Picture of Colored Men," New York *Citizen*, August 5, 1865. *Principia and National Era*, June 29, 1865.

7. New York *Tribune*, November 25, 1864. "Mass Meeting at Cooper Institute, January 3, 1865," in *The Freedman's Journal*, February 1865.

8. Garnet to Delany, February 1877, in Delany's *Autobiography*, quoted in Victor Ullmann, *Martin R. Delany: The Beginnings of Black Nationalism* (Boston, 1971).

9. Benjamin Quarles, *Black Abolitionists* (New York, 1969).

10. Alessandra Lorini, *Rituals of Race* (Charlottesville, Va., 1999). *The Diary of George Templeton Strong*, March 6, 1865.

11. *National Celebration of Union Victories, March 6th, 1865* (New York, 1865).

12. *Frank Leslie's Illustrated Newspaper*, May 6, 1865. *Strong Diary*, May 4, 1865.

13. "Obsequies of the Martyred President," *National Anti-Slavery Standard*, April 29, 1865.

3: Toward Reconstruction

1. *Walt Whitman's Drum-Taps* (New York, 1865).

2. *Nation*, July 6, 1865.

3. Ibid; *Nation*, February 2, 1866.

4. "The Paradise of Mediocrities," *Nation*, July 13, 1865. "The Week," *Nation*, March 8, 1866.

5. "A Society for Improving . . . ," *Nation*, September 28, 1865.

6. Godkin letter to Charles Eliot Norton, February 28, 1865, in Rollo Ogden, ed., *Life and Letters of Edwin Lawrence Godkin* vol. 1 (New York, 1907), 46. "Topics of the Day," *Nation*, June 17, 1866. "The Public Library," *Nation*, June 25, 1866. Another pet project of Godkin's was the reform of West Point. He called attention to the politicized admissions process and lax standards at the military academy. "The West Point Military Academy," *Nation*, December 28, 1865.

7. "Bayonets and School-Houses," *Nation*, January 18, 1866. "Class Rule," *Nation*, August 3, 1865. "The Reconstruction Discussion," *Nation*, May 21, 1866. "The Latest Phase of Conservatism," *Nation*, August 31,

1865. Godkin quoted in John J. Clancy, Jr., "A Mugwump on Minorities," *Journal of Negro History* 51 (July 1966), 181.

8. "The Sanitary Commission . . . ," *Nation*, August 24, 1865. Godkin was uncharacteristically optimistic in an April letter to Frederick Law Olmsted: "All difficulty is I think now over; I mean all alarming difficulty—military, political, and financial. Though I confess I would be very anxious about the terms of reconstruction, if Lincoln were not to be president for the next four years." Of course, before the week ended, Godkin had plenty of reason to grow pessimistic over the future course of Reconstruction. Godkin letter #1201 to Olmsted, April 12, 1865, Godkin Papers, Houghton Library, Harvard University. Sven Beckert, *The Monied Metropolis* (New York, 2001). "Club Life," *Nation*, July 6, 1865.

9. "To the Honorary Council of the Citizens' Association of New York," March 19, 1866, 8.

10. "The Republic Hereafter," New York *Citizen*, March 18, 1865. Citizens' Association of New York, *Our City Government*, January 25, 1864, 4.

11. Council of Hygiene and Public Health of the Citizens' Association of New York, *Report of the Council of Hygiene and Public Health of the Citizens' Association of New York upon the Sanitary Condition of the City* (New York, 1866), hereafter cited as *Sanitary Report. Frank Leslie's Illustrated Newspaper*, July 1, 1865.

12. The group's work is compiled in the published *Sanitary Report*. Individual journals and other unpublished records of the inspectors are at the New-York Historical Society (NYHS). Sanitary Commission of the Citizens' Association Recordbooks, Book 1, 29, 119; Book 6, 4, NYHS.

13. Charles E. Rosenberg, *The Cholera Years: The United States in 1832, 1849 and 1866* (Chicago, 1962), 193. "The Week," *Nation*, March 29, 1866.

14. "Our City Government," 3. "An Appeal by the Citizens' Association of New York," 28.

15. "Wholesale Corruption," "Our Taxes, Markets, Streets, and Sanitary Condition," among other titles. "Important Reform Measures," 1866, 12.

16. "The Citizens' Association and the Corporation Laborers," *Irish American*, January 14, 1864. *Workingmen's Advocate*, January 21, 1865.

17. "Our Streets," New York *Tribune*, February 1, 1865.

18. "Political Parties and their places of meeting in New York City," Thomas E. V. Smith, presented to the New-York Historical Society, February 7, 1893. Kilroe Collection, Box 24, Butler Library, Columbia University.

19. Kilroe Collection of Tammaniana, Butler Library, Columbia University. Iver Bernstein's *The New York City Draft Riots* is the definitive account of Tammany-style nationalism.

20. *Restoration and Peace! National Union Celebration at Union Square* (New York, 1866), 1.

21. See Tilden's drafts of the speech, Tilden Papers, Box 16, New York Public Library (NYPL).

22. Alexander C. Flick, *Samuel Jones Tilden: A Study in Political Sagacity* (New York, 1939).

23. Tilden letter declining to take part in March 6 celebration of Union army victories, March 3, 1865, Tilden Papers, Box 6, NYPL. Tilden's remarks to Tammany's July 4 celebration, 1866, Tilden Papers, NYPL.

24. New York *Herald*, October 31, 1866. Jean H. Baker, *Affairs of Party: The Political Culture of Northern Democrats in the Mid-Nineteenth Century* (Ithaca, N.Y., 1983).

4: An Age of Conventions

1, On the Thirteenth Amendment, see Michael Vorenberg, *Final Freedom* (New York, 2001).

2. *Congressional Globe*, First Session, Thirty-ninth Congress, 14.

3. *Congressional Globe*, Thirty-ninth Congress, 46.

4. John Chanler, *This Is a White Workingman's Government* (Washington, D.C., 1866).

5. *National Anti-Slavery Standard*, October 27, 1866. For the decades-long struggle against racially discriminatory property qualifications, see David N. Gellman and David Quigley, *Jim Crow New York: A Documentary History of Race and Citizenship, 1777–1877* (New York, 2003).

6. Henry C. Bellows, *Historical Sketch of the Union League Club* (New York, 1879), 79. As the New York convention met, Michigan and Maryland were simultaneously revising their own constitutions. Leaders of the various state conventions were in contact with each other. See New York (State) Constitutional Convention, *Journal of the Convention of the State of New York* (Albany, 1867), 73. Republicans were not alone in politicizing the proposed convention, as New York Democrats voiced reservations about the possibility. Tammany Hall's organ, the *Freeman's Journal*, regularly denounced those who sought a convention, asserting "this is no proper time for any State, in this so-called Union, to revise its fundamental Constitution." *Freeman's Journal and Catholic Register*, May 4, 1867, and June 22, 1867.

7. Dr. William Henry Johnson, *The Autobiography of Dr. William Henry Johnson* (Albany, 1900), 70. "State of New York Colored Citizens Central State Committee," June 17, 1867. Petition presented to the State Constitutional Convention, Political Broadsides Collection, New York State Library (NYSL).

8. Charles Z. Lincoln, *The Constitutional History of New York* vol. 2 (Rochester, 1906), 241. James C. Mohr, *The Radical Republicans and Reform in New York during Reconstruction* (Ithaca, N.Y., 1973), 210.

9. *Journal of the Assembly of the State of New York* (Albany, 1867), 439–440. The 160 delegates were to be selected as follows: four from each of the state's 32 senate districts (128 total) plus 32 delegates elected from the state at large. Each individual voter in the state could vote for sixteen of the at-large candidates. In addition, voters were required to take a loyalty oath. *Journal of the Convention*, 3, 12–13.

10. *Journal of the Convention*, 17, 26. Unfortunately, delegate L. Harris Hiscock died overnight, forcing early adjournment of the convention's first full day of business.

11. See the early weeks of the convention, *Journal of the Convention*.

12. Mohr, *The Radical Republicans and Reform in New York*, 222–223. *Documents of the Convention*, number 12.

13. Gellman and Quigley, *Jim Crow New York*.

14. Greeley letter to Mrs. R. M. Whipple, April 13, 1865; Greeley letter to Lorena Borde, February 4, 1866; Greeley letter to James Lawrence, December 16, 1866, Greeley Papers, Library of Congress.

15. "Report of the Committee on the Right of Suffrage and Qualifications to Hold Office," *Documents of the Convention*, number 15.

16. Ibid. George William Curtis spent much of the summer of 1867 criticizing Greeley for opting to reject women's suffrage. See George William Curtis, *Equal Rights for Women: A Speech by George William Curtis in the Constitutional Convention of New York, at Albany, July 19, 1867* (Boston, 1869).

17. Greeley letter to Rebekah M. Whipple, July 11, 1867, Greeley Papers, Library of Congress. Minority Report, Tilden Papers, NYPL. *Documents of the Convention*, number 16.

18. *Documents of the Convention*, number 16.

19. "Citizens' Association of New York, *The Constitutional Convention. The Metropolitan Commissions, Expenses, etc.* (New York, 1867), 5. *The Constitutional Convention. The Basis or General Plan . . .* (New York, 1867), 4.

20. "The Right of Suffrage," New York *Citizen*, September 7, 1867. *Documents of the Convention*, number 17.

21. Simon Sterne of the Personal Representation Society, *Report to the Constitutional Convention* (New York, 1867), 39.

22. *Freeman's Journal*, July 20, 1867, and January 4, 1868.

23. Greeley letter to Robert Bouner of New York City, August 7, 1867, Greeley papers, Library of Congress. New York *World*, September 26 and 27, 1867. "The State Convention," New York *Citizen*, August 31, 1867.

24. "The Late Elections," New York *Citizen*, October 19, 1867. "The Elections," *Irish Citizen*, October 19, 1867. Ohio, Pennsylvania, and Indiana were all sites of Democratic victories. *Alarm Bell of Liberty*, October 1867.

25. "New York City: Democratic Rejoicings," *Irish Citizen*, October 19, 1867.

26. "The Elections," New York *Herald*, November 6, 1867. William Cassidy letter to Tilden, November 12, 1867, Tilden Papers, Box 6, NYPL. On Rynders, see Tyler Anbinder, *Five Points* (New York, 2001).

27. "The State Legislature," New York *Citizen*, January 11, 1868. Cassidy letter to Tilden, November 12, 1867, Tilden Papers, Box 6, NYPL. Obituary of Greeley, New York *Times*, November 30, 1872.

28. A. R. Lawrence, Jr., speech on January 28, 1868, *The Government of Cities* (New York, 1868).

29. Ibid.

30. Tilden letter of February 28, 1868, Tilden Papers, Box 6, NYPL.

31. Republican Campaign Tract from 1868, in Kilroe Ephemera, Kilroe Collection of Tammaniana, Butler Library, Columbia University. *Leader*, July 15, 1868. Van Evrie to Seymour, June 1868, Box 8, Seymour Papers, NYSL. See *Niggerhead and Blue Law Advocate*, a Democratic campaign pamphlet in 1868 that mocked African Americans in New York, NYHS. Samuel Barlow letter to Tilden, September 21, 1868, Tilden Papers, Box 6, NYPL.

32. *Proceedings of the National Convention of the Colored Men of America* (Washington, D.C., 1869).

33. New York State Colored Citizens Central Committee, "Call for a State Convention," March 1869, Political Broadsides Collection, NYSL.

34. *Broome [County] Republican and Standard*, June 2, 1869. The local Binghamton paper contained the best record of the convention's proceedings. Manhattan's daily press made little mention of the meeting.

35. "An Appeal to Christians," *National Anti-Slavery Standard*, November 6, 1869.

36. Ibid.

37. *The Tribune Almanac and Political Register for 1870* (New York, 1871).

5: Acts of Enforcement

1. Phyllis Field has argued that white New Yorkers came to accept equal manhood suffrage "from force of habit." Such an interpretation neglects the primary role played by federal force in 1870 and for the next quarter of a century. Phyllis Field, *The Politics of Race in New York* (Ithaca, N.Y., 1982), 219.

2. One of the best studies of politics in late-nineteenth-century Manhattan strangely neglects the federal role in the metropolis, focusing instead on state and city governments. David Hammack, *Power and Society: Greater New York at the Turn of the Century* (New York, 1982), 6.

3. Gillette, *Retreat from Reconstruction* (New York, 1979), 49.

4. *Nation*, February 10, 1870, 83.

5. "Close the Books!" New York *Tribune*, April 8, 1870, 4.

6. "Rejoicings in New York," *New Era*, April 14, 1870, 2.

7. "The Enfranchised Rejoicing," New York *Herald*, April 9, 1870; New York *Times*, April 9, 1870. See also Alessandra Lorini, *Rituals of Race: American Public Culture and the Search for Racial Democracy* (Charlottesville, Va., 1999), 24–26.

8. Rev. William F. Butler chaired the planning committee. Also involved were John N. Carney, Reverend Dr. Tarpin, Joseph Walker, Jacob Stewart, and E.V.C. Eato. See *National Anti-Slavery Standard*, February and March, 1870. New York *Tribune*, New York *Herald*, New York *Times*, New York *Sun*, April 9, 1870.

9. See Harvey Strum "Property Qualifications and Voting Behavior in New York, 1807–1816," *Journal of the Early Republic* 1 (1981), 347–371.

10. Republican State Committee, "Naturalization Frauds!" October 27, 1868, in Broadsides, New York State Library.

11. Breen, *Thirty Years of New York Politics*, 318.

12. See "A Memorial of a Committee of the Union League Club of the City of New York," presented to Congress, December 14, 1868, in Union League Club Library. Also noted in *Lawrence Committee Report*, 1.

13. *Lawrence Committee Report*, 160. See the hundreds of pages of testimony and data compiled by Davenport.

14. U.S. Congress, House of Representatives, Select Committee on Alleged New York Election Frauds, *Alleged New York Election Frauds*, Report No. 31, 40th Cong., 3d Sess., February 24, 1869 (hereafter referred to as *Lawrence Committee Report*), 1.

15. *U.S. Statutes at Large*, vol. XVI, 140.

16. Albie Burke's otherwise fine study of federal regulation of elections in the Gilded Age is limited by his unwillingness to make connections between the Southern and Northern dimensions of Reconstruction. Burke views Sections 19 and 20 as "out of character with the rest of the bill." Burke, "Federal Regulation of Congressional Elections in Northern Cities, 1871–1894," Ph.D. Dissertation, University of Chicago, 1968, 57.

17. Davenport, 71.

18. United States, *Congressional Globe*, 41st Cong., 2nd Sess., 1870, 3663.

19. Ibid, 3664.

20. Robert J. Kaczorowski, *The Politics of Judicial Interpretation* (New York, 1985), 79.

21. Conkling in *Congressional Globe*, 41st Cong., 2nd Sess., 1870, 5149, quoted in Burke, "Federal Regulation . . . ," 66.

22. William Gillette, *Retreat from Reconstruction*, 25.

23. Burke, "Federal Regulation . . . ," 3.

24. "The National Interest in the New York Election," *Harper's Weekly*, October 22, 1870, 674.

25. U.S. Congress, Committee on the Expenditures in the Department of Justice, *Expenditures in the Department of Justice: The Secret Service Fund*, Report No. 800, 44th Cong., 1st Sess., August 5, 1876 (hereafter referred to as the *Caulfield Committee Report*), 43. Davenport's youth was spent in the Protestant reform world of antebellum Brooklyn; his pastor was Henry Ward Beecher. Robert Anderson Horn, "National Control of Congressional Elections," Ph.D. Dissertation, Princeton University, 1942, 189.

26. *Caulfield Committee Report*, 140.

27. *Caulfield Committee Report*, 45; Burke, "Federal Regulation . . . ," 202.

28. *The Papers of Ulysses S. Grant*, Grant to Metcalf, October 19, 1870. Grant to Cox, October 20, 1870.

29. Attorney Gen. Amos T. Akerman recalled that "in the month of October and perhaps in November, in the year 1870, there were frequent conversations with the President, in which the frauds which were likely to be practiced [in New York City] were very frequently discussed." *Caulfield Committee Report*, 65. The Cabinet met for three hours on October 28 to discuss the election laws and "particularly as to New York." *Journal of Commerce*, October 29, 1870, 3.

30. Gillette, *Retreat from Reconstruction*, 387.

31. National Archives, Record Group 60, Department of Justice, Attorney

General Papers, *Letters Received from the Southern District of New York*, Sharpe to Attorney Gen. Akerman, October 10, 1870.

32. See Burke, "Federal Regulation . . . ," 77.

33. *Journal of Commerce*, October 29, 1870.

34. "An Unfortunate Precedent," *Journal of Commerce*, October 31, 1870, 2.

35. "The Congressional Election Law," New York *Evening Post*, October 29, 1870, 4. "The Election Law," *Evening Post*, October 31, 1870, 3.

36. "The Federal Inspection of the Election," *Journal of Commerce*, November 1, 1870, 2.

37. *New National Era*, November 3, 1870.

38. "Wall Street Meetings," *Journal of Commerce*, October 12, 1870.

39. C. W. Seaton, Superintendent of the Census, *Census of the State of New York for 1875. Compiled from the Original Returns . . .* (Albany, 1877), 2.

40. See Allen W. Trelease, *White Terror: The Ku Klux Klan Conspiracy and Southern Reconstruction* (New York, 1971).

41. New York *World*, October 30, 1870. These charges were picked up by other metropolitan dailies and were cited by congressmen as late as 1881. See Burke, "Federal Regulation . . . ," 216–221.

42. "The Men Who Are to Give Us Honest Elections," New York *Sun*, October 31, 1870.

43. Davenport, *New York Election Frauds . . .* , 321–325. See also Police Court Docket Books, October and November 1870, New York City Municipal Archives.

44. New York *Evening Post*, November 1, 1870, 3.

45. John I. Davenport, *The Election and Naturalization Frauds in New York City, 1860–1870*, vol. I (New York, 1881), 321–322.

46. *Journal of Commerce*, late October 1870.

47. New York *Times*, November 9, 1870.

48. Davenport, 322–323.

49. "The Election Law," New York *Evening Post*, November 8, 1870.

50. *Journal of Commerce*, October 26, 1870.

51. New York *Evening Post*, November 2, 1870, 3.

52. Woodruff's opinion in *U.S. v Quinn*, in Frederick C. Brightly, *A Collection of Leading Cases on the Law of Elections in the United States . . .* (Philadelphia, 1871), 592.

53. See Gillette, *Retreat from Reconstruction*, 387, footnote 44, for a lengthy discussion of the Grant administration's special interest in New York City in the fall of 1870.

54. "Federal Preparations," New York *Times*, November 8, 1870, 1.

55. *The Diary of George Templeton Strong*, October 27, 1870.
56. Breen, 329. Writing in 1899, Breen compared the Enforcement Acts with the Alien and Sedition Acts of the late eighteenth century. Ibid, 408.
57. "An Unfortunate Precedent," *Journal of Commerce*, October 31, 1870, 2.
58. "Election Day," *Journal of Commerce*, November 8, 1870, 2.
59. "The Federal Invasion of New York," *Journal of Commerce*, October 26, 1870, 2.
60. "The Election," New York *Evening Post*, November 7, 1870, 4.
61. *Journal of Commerce*, November 8, 1870. New York *Times*, November 9, 1870, 1.
62. "The Election," New York *Evening Post*, November 8, 1870, 2. George Templeton Strong credited the federal military presence with keeping the peace: "election seems to have gone off peacefully, thanks to the federal bayonets that have been snuggly stowed away out of sight at various points in and around the city." *The Diary of George Templeton Strong*, November 8, 1870.
63. "The Election," New York *Evening Post*, November 8, 1870, 3.
64. Ibid.
65. Ibid.
66. *Journal of Commerce*, November 9, 1870, 3.
67. New York *Times*, November 9, 1870.
68. New York *World*, November 10, 1870.
69. *The Papers of Ulysses S. Grant*, Grant to Davenport, March 2, 1871.
70. Robert J. Kaczorowski, *The Politics of Judicial Interpretation*, chapter 4. Foner, *Reconstruction*, 455–459.
71. *Caulfield Committee Report*, ix.
72. *Caulfield Committee Report*, 18.
73. *Caulfield Committee Report*, 42.
74. U.S. Congress, House of Representatives, *Expenditures for Supervisors and Deputy Marshals at Elections, 1870–1884*, 48th Cong., 2d. Ex., Doc. 247; Burke, 108.
75. Burke, "Federal Regulation . . . ," ii. At the same time, the precarious nature of the federal presence in New York City in the 1870s must be emphasized. Davenport ran his staff of supervisors and special deputy marshals out of his home at 143 East 37th Street. *Caulfield Committee Report*, 25. As Davenport fell into thousands of dollars of debt in his work for the federal government, he turned to numerous local Republicans for financial support. The Union League Club, collector of the New

York Customs House Chester Arthur, and U.S. Marshal George Sharpe all contributed to Davenport's work. *Caulfield Committee Report*, 46.

6: Liberty and the Postwar City

1. Entries for June 3, 1870, and December 7, 1870, Emma Waite Diary, Special Collections, New York State Library (NYSL).
2. Entries for November 1, 1870, and December 31, 1870, Waite Diary, NYSL.
3. For recent attempts to reintroduce the category of caste into American thought, see John U. Ogbu, *Minority Education and Caste* (New York, 1978); Benjamin DeMott, *The Trouble with Friendship: Why Americans Can't Think Straight About Race* (New York, 1995).
4. Influential in my thinking about keywords are Raymond Williams, *Keywords: A Vocabulary of Culture and Society* (New York, 1976), and Daniel T. Rogers, *Contested Truths: Keywords in American Politics Since Independence* (New York, 1987).
5. On liberty, see Sir Isaiah Berlin, *Four Essays on Liberty* (London, 1969). John G. Sproat, *"The Best Men": Liberal Reformers in the Gilded Age* (New York, 1968).
6. Herbert G. Gutman, "The Tompkins Square 'Riot' in New York City on January 13, 1874: A Re-examination of Its Causes and Its Aftermath," *Labor History* 6 (Winter 1965), 44–70.
7. Seymour Mandelbaum, *Boss Tweed's New York*, 71, 72.
8. Philip M. Katz, *From Appomattox to Montmartre: Americans and the Paris Commune* (Cambridge, Mass., 1998). Timothy Messer-Kruse, *The Yankee International: Marxism and the American Reform Tradition, 1848–1876* (Chapel Hill, 1998). Henry Ammon James, *Communism in America* (New York, 1879).
9. E. L. Godkin, "'The Commune' and the Labor Question," *Nation*, May 18, 1871.
10. Michael A. Gordon characterizes the events of July 1871 as "a militia riot perpetrated by political reformers and men of property whose views reflected ethnic and class interests more than they did party affiliations." Michael A. Gordon, *The Orange Riots: Irish Political Violence in New York City, 1870 and 1871* (Ithaca, N.Y., 1993), 151.
11. Gordon, *The Orange Riots*, 4. New York *Times*, July 12, 1871. New York *Tribune*, July 18, 1871. Joel Tyler Headley, *The Great Riots of New York City, 1712–1873* (New York, 1873), 305.
12. Morton Keller, *The Art and Politics of Thomas Nast* (New York, 1965).

13. Tilden Circular for the Committee of Seventy, Tilden Papers, Box 22, New York Public Library (NYPL). Tilden letter to Robert Minturn, August 12, 1871, Tilden Papers, Box 7, NYPL. Tilden speech to Committee of Seventy at Cooper Union, November 2, 1871, Tilden Papers, Box 16, NYPL.
14. Gordon, *The Orange Riots*, 195.
15. Greeley to Mrs. C. D. Whipple, December 30, 1869, Papers of Horace Greeley, Container 1, Library of Congress. Nathan Greeley, "A Bibliography of Horace Greeley," typescript, Greeley Papers, Library of Congress. List of medals, posters, etc., for Horace Greeley's 1872 Campaign, Greeley Letters, New-York Historical Society (NYHS).
16. Horace Greeley speech, "The Colored Race," delivered at Poughkeepsie, May 16, 1872, Greeley Papers, Box 5, Scrapbook 1, Library of Congress. The speech's announced topics included "The African in America—His Opportunities and His Responsibilities—The Question of Equality—The Duty of Self-Trust—Noble Example of the Jews—An Exhortation to Thrift."
17. Ibid.
18. Samuel Wright to Horace Greeley, June 3, 1872, Greeley Papers, Box 7, Library of Congress. Forrest G. Wood argued that the 1872 election signaled "the Decline of the Race Issue." It was a partial and only temporary decline in Manhattan; linked to the decline of race was the emergence of class in the form of an emboldened bourgeois reform movement. Forrest G. Wood, *Black Scare: The Racist Response to Emancipation and Reconstruction* (Berkeley, 1868).
19. Horace Greeley to Gabrielle M. Greeley, July 28, 1872; Greeley to R. M. Whipple, October 18, 1872; Greeley to Margaret Allen, November 4, 1872, Greeley Papers, Container 1, Library of Congress.
20. New York *Herald*, December 12, 13, 1873.
21. "Governor's Message," New York *Tribune*, January 7, 1874.
22. "Laborers Crying for Work," New York *Tribune*, January 6, 1874. The classic study of the events is Herbert Gutman, "The Failure of the Movement by the Unemployed for Public Works in 1873," *Political Science Quarterly* 80 (June 1965), 254–276.
23. Circular issued by the Committee of Safety, January 6, 1874.
24. New York *Tribune*, January 13, 1874.
25. John Swinton, *The Tompkins Square Outrage* (Albany, 1874). Herbert Gutman, "The Tompkins Square 'Riot' . . ."
26. New York *Tribune*, January 13, 1874.

7: Tilden's America

1. Samuel J. Tilden, Formal Letter of Acceptance, July 31, 1876, printed as "Reform," Tilden Papers, Box 47, New York Public Library (NYPL).
2. Annual Message, 1874, *Annual Messages of the Governor*.
3. E. L. Godkin, "Criminal Politics," *North American Review* 150 (1890), 706–723. For general accounts of the Tweed years, see Seymour Mandelbaum, *Boss Tweed's New York* (New York, 1965); Alexander B. Callow, Jr., *The Tweed Ring* (New York, 1966); Burrows and Wallace, *Gotham: A History of New York City to 1898* (New York, 1999).
4. See John Sproat, *"The Best Men": Liberal Reformers in the Gilded Age* (New York, 1968); Iver Bernstein, *The New York City Draft Riots* (New York, 1990); Thomas Bender, *New York Intellect* (New York, 1987); Michael E. McGerr, *The Decline of Popular Politics* (New York, 1986).
5. Eric Foner, *Reconstruction: America's Unfinished Revolution, 1863–1877* (New York, 1988), 569; letter from William D. Porter, South Carolina Democratic leader, to various Southern newspapers before national Democratic convention in 1876, June 21, 1876, Tilden Papers, Box 9, NYPL; "Tilden Bewildered," New York *Times*, October 29, 1877.
6. Tilden interview with William Howard, November 27, 1875, Tilden Papers, Box 16, NYPL.
7. Seymour speech to the New York State Democratic convention in Syracuse, September 16, 1874, in Political Scrapbook #22, Volume 13, 1870–1878, Seymour Collection, New York State Library (NYSL).
8. Foner, *Reconstruction*, 523. "Advice to Voters," New York *Sun*, November 2, 1874.
9. Tilden speech to the New York State Democratic Party in Syracuse, September 17, 1874, Tilden Papers, Box 16, NYPL.
10. Ibid. See other campaign speeches from the fall of 1874, Tilden Papers, Box 16, NYPL.
11. Ibid.
12. Thurlow Weed, "An Appeal to the Public," October 31, 1874, encapsulated many of his criticisms from the 1874 campaign season, in Tilden Papers, Box 47, NYPL. Evidence of such attacks on Tilden's wartime record also appeared in the New York *Sun*, November 2, 1874.
13. See David Blight's landmark study of postbellum memory, *Race and Reunion: The Civil War in American Memory* (Cambridge, Mass., 2001). William Havermeyer letter to Edwin Morgan, August 13, 1874, Morgan Collection, Box 6, NYSL. Havermeyer was another Democrat who ef-

fectively charted a career as an anti-Tammany reformer in the 1870s. In this letter, he attacked the city's Democratic Party but then tells the Republican senator that "I am now and always have been, and always expect to be, a member of the Democratic Party." William Allen Butler letter to Samuel J. Tilden, September 18, 1874, Tilden Papers, Box 8, NYPL.

14. Samuel Jones Tilden, *The New York city 'Ring': its origin, maturity and fall* . . . (New York, 1873), 6. "Reception of the Young Democratic Club," New York *World*, November 20, 1874.

15. Resolution of the Merchants of New York City at the Chamber of Commerce, December 8, 1875. Alexander Stewart letter to Tilden, December 16, 1875, Tilden Papers, Box 19, NYPL. Governor Tilden, Message on Railroad Transportation, 1875, Tilden Papers, Box 19, NYPL. Tilden's closest friends remarked on how the new governor could not help but maintain an active interest in his business involvements. In his first weeks in Albany, one associate noted that, "Mr. Tilden expressed himself much dissatisfied with the present condition of the mines' business." George Smith letter to W. L. Westmore, January 18, 1875, Tilden Papers, Letterbook Volume 7, NYPL. While defining a procorporation program of reform, Tilden was careful to maintain some traditional Democratic support among the working-class voters of the state. He appealed to urban workers when vetoing a convict labor bill in early 1876. A Democratic ward association in New York City praised the governor "for the great interest he exhibited in behalf of the working men of this state." Letter from the James Daly Association of the Thirteenth Assembly District, March 1876, Tilden Papers, Box 20, NYPL.

16. For an example of the national scope of this movement, see Col. Richard Lathers, *South Carolina, Her Wrongs and the Remedy, Delivered to the Opening of the Taxpayers' Convention in Columbia, S.C., February 17, 1874* (Charleston, 1874), found in Tilden Papers, Box 8, NYPL. Southern whites typically called for the end to federal Reconstruction in the language of taxpayers' rights and the need for retrenchment. Interestingly, Tilden kept this pamphlet in his personal papers and borrowed from its rhetoric in many of his later speeches and messages. *Tilden Commission Report*, 1. A survey of state and national debt throughout the nineteenth century is in the Tilden Papers, Box 12, NYPL. Tilden was obsessed with the growth of public debt, constantly commenting on the subject in his notes. "The Government of Cities," New York *Times*, April 8, 1877.

17. Tilden's Annual Message, 1876, 52; unsigned statement, 1876; Tilden undated statement, Tilden Papers, Box 19, NYPL.

18. Proposed city charter, 1872, and "Unconstitutionality of the Charter of the Committee of Seventy," Tilden Papers, Box 24, NYPL. This proposed suffrage reform is strikingly similar to recent controversial proposals of Lani Guinier. Where such measures are intended to protect racial and ethnic minorities today, in the nineteenth century they were designed to maintain elite control of politics. The contrast between the two moments underscores the highly variable nature of American liberal thought. Lani Guinier, *The Tyranny of the Majority: Fundamental Fairness and Representative Democracy* (New York, 1994).

19. See McGerr, *The Decline of Popular Politics*, chapter 3. Charles Francis Adams, Jr., "The Protection of the Ballot in National Elections," *Journals of Social Science* 1 (1869), 106; Dorman B. Eaton, "Municipal Government," *Journal of Social Science* 5 (1873), 7. On the growing fear of the sheer numbers of the urban poor, see Meyer Stern, "Local Self Government," New York *Times*, March 30, 1877.

20. Annual Message, 1875, in Charles Z. Lincoln, *The Constitutional History of New York* vol. 2 (Rochester, 1906), 668.

21. "Special Message from the Governor," May 11, 1875, in *Documents of the Assembly of the State of New York, 98th Session—1875* (Albany, 1875), 1.

22. Lincoln, *Constitutional History* vol. 2, 669.

23. New York City Council on Political Reform, *Report of the New York City Council of Political Reform for the Years 1872, 1873, and 1874. With Summary* (New York, 1875), 5, 10. Alexander C. Flick, *Samuel Jones Tilden: A Study in Political Sagacity* (New York, 1939), 259–261. "Annual Message of the Governor, 1875," *Documents of the Assembly.* "Special Message of the Governor, May 11, 1875," *Documents of the Assembly* vol. 10, number 159. "The Municipal Message," New York *Sun*, May 12, 1875. Lincoln, *Constitutional History* vol. 2, 668–669. Letter from Assemblyman James Daly (Dem.), November 16, 1875, Tilden papers, Box 20, NYPL. Daly warned the governor that "it is definitely the intention of the Republican majority to offer a partisan charter next winter."

24. Martin B. Anderson, the president of the University of Rochester, was the only New Yorker to turn down Governor Tilden's request to serve on the commission. Lincoln, *Constitutional History* vol. 2, 669. Some members volunteered in the weeks after the governor's special message in May. William A. Butler letter to Tilden, May 28, 1875, Tilden Papers, Box 19, NYPL. Samuel Hand letter to Tilden, November 13, 1875,

Tilden Papers, Box 19, NYPL. Henry Dimock letter to Tilden, December 1, 1875, Tilden Papers, Box 20, NYPL.

25. "City and County Affairs," *Irish World*, December 25, 1875. E. L. Godkin, for one, reported feeling sick at the first meeting of the commission and returned to Cambridge, Massachusetts, "in a low state." Godkin to F. L. Olmsted, December 17, 1875, Olmsted Papers, Library of Congress.

26. Godkin to W. P. Garrison, May 5, 1875, #1070, Godkin Papers, Houghton Library, Harvard University. Godkin promised "to endeavor to discharge the duties of the office to the best of my ability." Godkin to Tilden, December 2, 1875, Tilden Papers, Box 20, NYPL. Godkin to Olmsted, November 16, 1875, Olmsted Papers, Library of Congress.

27. Thomas Bender, *New York Intellect*, 184.

28. Sterne to Tilden, May 14, 1875, and Sterne to Tilden, April 6, 1876, Tilden Papers, Box 20, NYPL.

29. New York *Staats Zeitung*, February 15 and 27, 1875.

30. For a comprehensive biography and a major reinterpretation, see Joan Waugh, *Unsentimental Reformer: The Life of Josephine Shaw Lowell* (Cambridge, Mass., 1997).

31. *Tenth Annual Report of the State Board of Charities* (Albany, 1877). *Report on the Subject of Vagrancy*, submitted at a meeting of the State Board of Charities, held December 4, 1877, 1, NYSL. Amy Dru Stanley, *From Bondage to Contract* (New York, 1998) is a masterful study of the discourse of *vagrants* and *tramps* in the 1870s North.

32. Ibid. Commissioner Edward C. Donnelly of New York City dissented, criticizing the idea of a statewide system of workhouses on the grounds of local control: "a fundamental principle of our political system, local independence and individuality."

33. "Saratoga Conference Applying Scientific Analysis to the Problems of Human Society," New York *Sun*, September 6, 1876.

34. Godkin to Charles Eliot Norton, July 14, 1876, in William M. Armstrong, ed., *The Gilded Age Letters of E. L. Godkin* (Albany, 1974), 238–239. Tilden letter of acceptance to the Democratic National Convention, July 11, 1876, Tilden Papers, Box 47, NYPL.

35. Platform of the Democratic Party, 1876, Tilden Papers, Box 47, NYPL. Samuel Tilden, "Reform!" July 31, 1876, Tilden Papers, Box 47, NYPL.

36. Tilden campaign speech, October 1876, Tilden Papers, Box 47, NYPL. See the effusive praise in the biography of Tilden in the Louisville,

Kentucky, *Courier-Journal*, April 1876. William D. Porter letters in unknown *Charleston* newspaper, June 21, 1876, Tilden Papers, Box 9, NYPL.

37. Ibid.

38. Numerous letters from Southern white supporters can be found in Boxes 9 and 10 of the Tilden Papers, NYPL. Iver Bernstein's *The New York City Draft Riots*, 63–66, 217, charts Tilden's politics during the Civil War and in the early years of Reconstruction, including the future governor's adamant stand against granting African Americans the vote at the 1867–1868 state constitutional convention.

39. William J. Best letter to Tilden, June 29, 1876, Tilden Papers, Box 9, NYPL. John Sproat, *"The Best Men,"* 101, locates a "resurgent whiggism" in both parties in 1876, as both Democrats and Republicans appealed to former Whigs in the South. One Republican loyalist complained that "the whole course of the paper has been to belittle Hayes while defending or lauding Tilden." Manning Ferguson Force to Godkin, October 23, 1876, #283, Godkin Papers, Houghton Library, Harvard University. W. F. Pelton of the Democratic National Committee, August 14, 1876, Seymour Collection, Box 11, NYSL. Letter from the James Daly Association of the Thirteenth Assembly District, March 1876, Tilden Papers, Box 20; Letter from Henry George, August 22, 1876; Letter from Ignatius Donnelly, August 28, 1876, Tilden Papers, Box 9, NYPL.

40. Resolutions of the James Daly Association of the Thirteenth Assembly District, July 10, 1876, Tilden Papers, Box 47, NYPL.

41. Seymour to William Wheeler, 47, Political Scrapbook #2, Seymour Collection, NYSL.

42. "Thoughts for Election Day," *Irish World*, November 4, 1876.

8: "The proud name of 'Citizen' has sunk"

1. "The Rights of Citizens," *Irish World*, August 25, 1877, 6. For a discussion of an earlier chapter in Devyr's long career as a transatlantic firebrand, see Jonathan Halperin Earle, "The Undaunted Democracy: Jacksonian Antislavery and Free Soil, 1828–1848," Ph.D. diss., Princeton University, 1996. My reading of the struggle over the suffrage in 1877 New York has been especially influenced by Judith Shklar's historically grounded liberalism. Judith N. Shklar, *American Citizenship: The Quest for Inclusion* (Cambridge, Mass., 1991).

2. Among the various accounts of the Tilden Commission, the best are Michael E. McGerr, *The Decline of Popular Politics: The American North, 1865–1928* (New York, 1986); Seymour Mandelbaum, *Boss Tweed's New York* (New York, 1965); Charles Z. Lincoln, *The Constitutional History of the State of New York: Volume Two* (Rochester, 1906), 659–673; Sven Beckert, *The Monied Metropolis*; and Roy Rosenzweig and Elizabeth Blackmar, *The Park and the People: A History of Central Park* (Ithaca, N.Y., 1992). The best account of the commission's legacies is David C. Hammack, *Power and Society: Greater New York at the Turn of the Century* (New York, 1982).

3. London *Daily Telegraph*, November 9, 1876.

4. Taylor letter to Tilden, November 14, 1876, Tilden Papers, Box 10, NYPL.

5. Keith Polakoff, *The Politics of Inertia: The Election of 1876 and the End of Reconstruction* (Baton Rouge, 1973); C. Vann Woodward, *Reunion and Reaction: The Compromise of 1877 and the End of Reconstruction* (Boston, 1951). Seymour speech to the New York State Electoral College, December 1876, Seymour Collection, Political Scrapbooks, Book 2, NYSL. "The New York Electors," Albany *Argus*, December 7, 1876.

6. Adams letter to Tilden, January 16, 1877, Tilden Papers, Box 11, NYPL.

7. Correspondence for 1877, Tilden Papers, NYPL.

8. Clarence Buel, *The Memoirs of Clarence Clough Buel, 1850–1933*, in Union League Club Library. "The Unemployed Workingmen," *The Irish American*, February 17, 1877. Numerous other petitions and meetings are documented in the *Times*, the *Sun*, and the *Evening Post*.

9. Foner, *Reconstruction*, 336. Chester L. Barrows, *William M. Evarts: Lawyer, Diplomat, Statesman* (Chapel Hill, 1941). Flick, *Samuel Jones Tilden*, 388. "The Electoral Tribunal," New York *Times*, February 6, 1877.

10. Evarts speech of February 15, 1877, quoted in "Victims of the Constitution," New York *Times*, April 15, 1877. "The Government of Cities," New York *Times*, April 8, 1877.

11. Evarts letters to Edwards Pierrepont (#668), March 6, 1877, and (#709) March 8, 1877; Astor to Evarts (#636), March 2, 1877; James Ridgeway to Evarts (#658), March 5, 1877; J. Thomson to Evarts (#920), March 24, 1877, Evarts Papers, Library of Congress.

12. For accounts of Evarts's role in the national strike wave, and his earlier involvement in the Jacobs case, see the *Labor Standard*, July and Au-

gust 1877. Each weekly report is punctuated by derogatory references to "Leech" Evarts. For the publication of the radical Workingmen's Party, William Evarts personified the oppressive policies of the nation's ruling class.

13. For an illuminating day-by-day account of the intersections of local and national politics in February 1877, see Tilden Papers, Box 11, NYPL. The "political crime" of the Electoral Commission was often denounced in the coming fall campaign. See New York *Times*, October 18, 1877. New York *Staats Zeitung*, February 22, 1877. "Tammany Frees Its Mind," New York *Tribune*, March 2, 1877.

14. George L. Prentiss, *Our National Bane; or, The Dry Rot in American Politics. A Tract for the Times Touching Civil Service Reform* (New York, 1877), 43.

15. New York *Times*, January 26, 1877.

16. *Tilden Commission Report*, 5. *Tilden Commission Report*, 25.

17. *Tilden Commission Report*, 3, 13, 14.

18. Ibid., 10.

19. Existing suffrage provisions would remain in effect for all other city elections—including mayoral and aldermanic—as well as state and national elections. *Tilden Commission Report*, 28.

20. "The Commission's Labors," New York *Times*, March 7, 1877.

21. "The Constitutional Amendments," New York *Times*, April 11, 1877, 4. Alongside Jacobs's principled opposition, the prominent Republican Roscoe Conkling abandoned the Tilden Commission by late 1877 for more practical political reasons. Conkling justified his party's eventual abandonment of the constitutional amendments by claiming that they were a "ridiculous thing, got up by Jackson Schultz and others, and a trap which [Republicans] would not touch." *Nation*, November 15, 1877, 294.

22. The shared interest of the taxpayers is key to understanding the workings of class in late-nineteenth- and early-twentieth-century America, especially in the cities. For the divided nature of Manhattan's elite, see Iver Bernstein, *The New York City Draft Riots*, and David C. Hammack, *Power and Society*.

23. Beckert, "The Making of New York City's Bourgeoisie, 1850–1886," (Ph.D. Diss., Columbia University, 1995), 323–329. *Nineteenth Annual Report of the Corporation of the Chamber of Commerce of the State of New-York for the Year 1876–77* (New York, 1877), 96–104.

24. Ibid. On April 2, a pro–Tilden Commission petition was circulated on

the floor of the Stock Exchange and was "extensively signed." Two days later, the Cotton Exchange held a special meeting of members on the floor at the close of business. James F. Morey concluded a speech in support of the proposed amendments by demanding of his fellow merchants, "We cannot fold our hands and look on, we must speak loudly now." New York *Times*, April 5, 1877. Before the first week of April was over, pro–Tilden Commission resolutions were passed by the Produce Exchange and the Importers' and Grocers' Board of Trade. New York *Times, Tribune, Sun, Evening Post*, April 8, 1877.

25. A mixture of careerist aspiration and firm antidemocratic belief fueled Sterne's yearlong campaign. Sterne would convert all of his hard work in 1877 into a role as a public expert on civil service reform and economic regulation for the remainder of the century. Letters from Sterne, Tilden Papers, Box 20, NYPL; John Foord, *The Life and Public Services of Simon Sterne* (London, 1903).

26. Simon Sterne, "The Administration of Cities," *The International Review* 4 (1877), 637–638.

27. "The Government of Cities," New York *Times*, June 6, 1877, 2; "The Government of Cities," New York *Times*, April 8, 1877, 1.

28. Sterne, "The Administration of Cities," 635.

29. Fatefully, on the same day that Senator Woodlin was celebrating the passage of his amendments in Albany, events were unfolding elsewhere that would shape the terms of the coming campaign. In Philadelphia, the board of directors of the Pennsylvania Railroad Company held an emergency meeting. The Board decided to institute a 10 percent pay cut in the wages and salaries of all employees making over one dollar per day. Tom Scott and his directors fired the first salvo in what turned out to be a nationwide, summer-long war between the railroads and their workers. The class conflict unleashed by the Pennsylvania Railroad on May 25 was to have a determining effect on the political struggle opened up by the Tilden Commission. New York *Times*, May 26, 1877. For the national scale of events in 1877, see Robert V. Bruce, *1877: Year of Violence* (Indianapolis, 1959); Richard Schneirov, *Labor and Urban Politics: Class Conflict and the Origins of Modern Liberalism in Chicago, 1864–1897* (Urbana, 1998); and David O. Stowell, *Streets, Railroads, and the Great Strike of 1877* (Chicago, 1999). In New York City, the New York State Convention of the Women's Suffrage Association was holding its annual meeting at Masonic Hall on May 25. The meeting covered the usual items of interest at such meetings: calls for a national

Sixteenth amendment for women's suffrage, support for sympathetic legislators, denunciations of opponents. This particular meeting grew heated at the discussion of Governor Robinson's veto of a bill that would have given women the right to sit on local school boards in New York. In her speech criticizing the governor, Matilda J. Gage argued that women should both be able to serve on local school boards and also to vote for those officials. Gage pointed to the Tilden Commission's proposals and suggested that property-holding women were more worthy of the franchise than the poor men of the state. Gage was the first of many unexpected New Yorkers who found common ground with the Tilden Commission's classist ideology. New York *Times* and New York *Tribune*, May 26, 1877.

30. New York *Sun*, April 8, 1877. "Disfranchisement," *Irish World*, April 28, 1877, 6.

31. New York *Times*, April 23, 1877. Timothy Messer-Kruse, *The Yankee International* (Chapel Hill, N.C., 1998). On the Paris Commune's influence on American political culture in the 1870s, see Philip Katz, *From Appommattox to Montmartre* (Cambridge, Mass., 1998).

32. "Declaration of Principles of the Workingmen's Party of the United States," in Philip S. Foner, *The Workingmen's Party of the United States: A History of the First Marxist Party in the Americas* (Minneapolis, 1984), 115–116.

33. Call for July 26 meeting at Cooper Institute in New York *Sun*, July 25, 1877. Dorothee Schneider, *Trade Unions and Community: The German Working Class in New York City, 1870–1900* (Urbana, Ill., 1994), 74. "The Voice of Labor," *Irish World*, August 4, 1877, 3; "Labor's Grievance," *Irish World*, August 4, 1877, 1.

34. On the night of July 24, a planning meeting for the Tompkins Square rally was held at Schwab's bar on the Bowery. Delegates from the Painters' Union Number Four, the Bookbinders' Union, the Artificial Flower Cooperative Union and the Paterson Silk Weavers were present. Schwab chaired the meeting and delivered a fiery address, reminding his colleagues of the violence of January 1874 in Tompkins Square. The German radical "urged that this time every man should be armed and ready to resist . . . You are American citizens and have a right to assemble peaceably." "The Voice of Labor," New York *Sun*, July 25, 1877, 1.

35. One colleague believed that "Schwab had a great deal to do with the making of John Swinton as a Socialist. It was he who probably showed

him around on the East Side of New York City." Robert Waters, *Career and Conversations of John Swinton, Journalist, Orator, Economist* (Chicago, 1902), 32. John Swinton, *A Momentous Question: The Respective Attitudes of Labor and Capital* (Philadelphia, 1895), chapter 17. New York *World* and New York *Sun*, July 27, 1877. Also John Swinton, *Striking for Life* (Philadelphia, 1895). "The Dreaded Assemblage," New York *Sun*, July 26, 1877, 3. In the wake of July's politicization, a diverse coalition of New Yorkers came together to oppose suffrage restriction. By the fall, the leading opposition to the Tilden Commission's Report came from Tammany Hall. All through 1877, Tammany fought against suffrage restrictions, both in the state legislature and in the wards of New York City. Defining the franchise as a "sacred right," Tammany maintained a steadfast policy "utterly opposed to any and all efforts to limit" that right. In the state Democratic Party's platform of 1877, Tammany's supporters included an explicit defense of the laboring class's right to vote. While rejecting Simon Sterne's vision of class-bound virtue, Tammany also attempted to reject the narrow nativist definitions of American identity offered by E. L. Godkin. The city's Democratic Party accused the proamendment forces of seeking "to prevent forever every one of foreign birth from becoming citizens of the United States." "The City Democracy," *Irish American*, November 10, 1877, 1; "Tammany Hall," *Irish American*, October 20, 1877, 4; "The Workingmen," *Irish American*, November 10, 1877, 4.

36. "City Government," *Nation*, October 25, 1877. "Criminal Politics," *North American Review* 150 (June 1890), 706–726. John Higham, *Strangers in the Land: Patterns of American Nativism, 1860–1925* (New Brunswick, N.J., 1955).

37. "The Rights of Taxpayers," *Harper's Weekly*, April 7, 1877; New York *Times*, September 8, 1877.

38. New York *Times*, May 14, 1877. On caste as the forgotten word in American history and politics, see George Fredrickson, "Far from the Promised Land," *New York Review of Books* 43 (April 18, 1996), 16–19.

39. Quote from Simon Sterne speech at the meeting, reported in New York *Times* account of the meeting. For descriptions of this meeting, see "Tax Payers Organizing," New York *Times*, October 23, 1877, 1; "Political Notes," *Labor Standard*, October 28, 1877; "A Peculiar Meeting to Support a Dangerous Scheme," New York *Sun*, October 22, 1877; "Shall the Very Poor Vote?" New York *Sun*, October 23, 1877; "The Issue of the Election," *Irish American*, November 3, 1877.

40. The "American citizen" quote comes from George W. Maddox, cited in New York *Sun*, October 23, 1877. On October 29, one week after the Steinway Hall confrontation, the largest rally of the campaign occurred in front of Tammany Hall. Typical of Reconstruction-era Tammany gatherings, the thousands who assembled were treated to several bands and an elaborate fireworks display. New York City's Democratic establishment all turned out; on the dais, the lieutenant governor, state legislators, the mayor, and countless minor Tammany officials presented themselves as a united front. Speeches were suffused with accusations of electoral fraud in 1876 and defenses of popular suffrage. With one week to go before the election, the Tammany Ring had made the defeat of the proposed constitutional amendments its only issue. "The City Democracy," *Irish American*, November 10, 1877, 1; "The Howling Democrats," New York *Times*, October 30, 1877, 8.

41. "Grand Uprising of the Cigar Makers in New York," *Cigar Makers' Official Journal*, October 15, 1877, 1; Schneider, *Trade Unions and Community: The German Working Class in New York City, 1870–1900*, 76–77.

42. Many of the radicals who disrupted the Steinway Hall rally on October 22 were members of the union. "The Striking Cigar Makers," New York *Times*, October 31, 1877, 8; *Labor Standard*, November 4, 1877, 1. For Gompers's general account of labor in the 1870s and the great strike of 1877, see Samuel Gompers, *Seventy Years of Life and Labor: An Autobiography* (New York, 1925), chapter 2.

43. "Labor Politics," *Labor Standard*, November 4, 1877, 2. Of all the combatants in the battle over the Tilden Commission, the Workingmen's Party came closest to articulating a consistently democratic vision of public life. The local New York section of the party fought for the principle that "the right of suffrage should be secured to every citizen of mature age, without regard to sex or condition." Invoking the spirit of John Brown, the *Labor Standard* called on all "wage slaves"—white and black—to rise up in defense of the people's vote. Few groups in 1877 were willing to go so far in their advocacy of popular suffrage. In the fall campaign, the Workingmen offered up the most inclusive vision of democratic citizenship. That this party—which would soon rename itself the Socialist Party—led the defense of equal rights in 1877 speaks to the strange career of American democracy. Workingmen's Party resolutions in "The Voice of Labor," *Irish World*, August 4, 1877, 3; "The White Slaves, John Brown 1859, The Workman 1877," *Labor Standard*, September 16, 1877, 3.

9: New York Reconstructed

1. Upstate Democrats successfully argued that an attack on the rights of the urban poor would easily lead to expanded property qualifications in rural areas. Charles Z. Lincoln, *Constitutional History of New York*, 660. "Albany, Meeting of the Legislature," New York *Times*, January 9, 1878, 1.

2. The national dimensions of this antidemocratic movement are discussed in John G. Sproat, *"The Best Men": Liberal Reformers in the Gilded Age* (New York, 1968).

3. Lincoln, *Constitutional History of New York*, 660. Taxpayers' Association of New York, *Review of the Legislation of 1877* (New York, 1878), 25.

4. *Nation*, October 25, 1877, 248. "Editorial," *Municipal Affairs*, 3 (September 1899), 395. Commission members such as William A. Butler, Simon Sterne, and E. L. Godkin wrote in the 1890s on the merits of suffrage restriction. Stern, in particular, crusaded to preserve the memory of the defeated 1877 campaign. James Bryce, *The American Commonwealth* (New York, 1888), 573–579. A more democratic wing of progressivism—at least in terms of urban politics—came to define itself against the memory of the Tilden Commission; see Woodrow Wilson, "Notes on Administration" (1890) in Arthur Link, ed., *The Papers of Woodrow Wilson* (vol. 6; Princeton, 1969), 484–521. For the best account of the varieties of American progressivism, see Daniel T. Rodgers, "In Search of Progressivism," *Reviews in American History* 10 (1982), 113–132.

5. Tilden letter to the Democratic Association of Massachusetts, February 21, 1880, Tilden Papers, Box 47, NYPL. Tilden letter to the New York State Delegation to the Democratic National Convention, June 18, 1880, Tilden Papers, Box 16, NYPL.

6. Godkin letter to Henry Cabot Lodge, February 15, 1880, Letter #479, Godkin Papers, Houghton Library, Harvard University. "Criminal Politics," *North American Review* 150 (June 1890), 706. For a similar attack on other elite reformers, see Henry Bellows, *History of the Union League Club* (New York, 1879), 162. Bellows concluded his account of the Union League Club's sixteen-year history by declaring that "if [we have] any function, it is certainly to battle with the faithlessness in American principle, which so easily affects our cultivated or easy class . . . It is not their [the poor's] activity but our sloth that causes most of the evils in American politics." E. L. Godkin to his son, Lawrence, July 12, 1894, *The Gilded Age Letters of E. L. Godkin*, 456.

7. Simon Sterne, *Suffrage in Cities* (New York, 1878), 35, 39. The lecture was part of a series offered at the Cooper Institute in the winter of 1877–1878.

8. Ibid.

9. Ibid. On the 1821 convention, and ensuing debates over the right of suffrage, see Gellman and Quigley, *Jim Crow New York*.

10. Simon Sterne, *The Railway Problem in the State of New York* . . . (New York, 1879). For his 1885 remarks, see Simon Sterne, manuscript of address entitled "Some Reflections on Recent Changes and Proposed Reforms in Legislation Affecting the City of New York," Sterne Papers, New York Public Library, cited in Hammack, *Power and Society*, 250. Burrows and Wallace, *Gotham: A History of New York City to 1898*, 1033. "Argument of Simon Sterne, Esq., Delivered at Albany, March 7, 1878. Before the Committee on Railroads, on 'Bill to create a Board of Railroad Commissioners, and to Regulate their Powers,'" Simon Sterne Pamphlets, New-York Historical Society (NYHS). See John Foord, *The Life and Public Service of Simon Sterne* (London, 1903); Ari Hoogenboom, *Outlawing the Spoils: A History of the Civil Service Reform Movement, 1865–1883* (Urbana, Ill., 1961). Simon Sterne, *Hindrances to Prosperity or Causes Which Retard Financial and Political Reforms in the United States* (New York, 1879).

11. William Allen Butler, *Our Great Metropolis: Its Growth, Misgovernment and Needs* (New York, 1880). Butler's lecture was delivered on February 6, 1879.

12. New York *Times*, February 20, 1879.

13. Roswell Dwight Hitchcock, *Socialism* (New York, 1879), 24, 41. Henry Ammon James, *Communism in America* (New York, 1879). Noel Ignatiev, *How the Irish Became White* (New York, 1995).

14. "The Tramp Nuisance," *Harper's Weekly*, December 1878. Michael B. Katz, *In The Shadow of the Poorhouse: A Social History of American Welfare* (New York, 1986), 67. Amy Dru Stanley, *From Bondage to Contract*.

15. Report of the 1878 Annual Meeting of the New York State Woman Suffrage Association, N.Y.W.S.A. Papers, Butler Library, Columbia University.

16. Emma Lou Thornbrough, *T. Thomas Fortune: Militant Journalist* (Chicago, 1972). "Easily the best black newspaper of the late nineteenth century." Georgette Merritt Campbell, *Extant Collections of Early Black Newspapers* (Troy, N.Y., 1981), xv. *Freeman's Journal*, the first African American newspaper in U.S. history, appeared in 1827. Franklin foreword in Thornbrough, *T. Thomas Fortune*, vii.

17. *John Swinton's Paper*, December 28, 1884.

18. Swinton, *A Momentous Question*, 237, 238.

19. John Swinton, *John Swinton's Travels: Current Views and Notes of Forty Days in France and England* (New York, 1880), 41.

Epilogue

1. Max Page, *The Creative Destruction of Manhattan, 1900–1940* (Chicago, 1999).

2. William S. McFeely, *Grant: A Biography* (New York, 1981), chapter 26.

3. William S. McFeely, "Ulysses S. Grant," in Alan Brinkley and Davis Dyer, *The Reader's Companion to the American Presidency* (Boston, 2000), 227.

4. New York *Times*, July 24, 1885.

5. David Blight, *Race and Reunion*, 216.

6. New York *Times*, July 29, 1885.

7. Michael Robert Mounter, "Richard Theodore Greener and the African American Individual in a Black and White World," in James Lowell Underwood and W. Lewis Burke, Jr., eds., *At Freedom's Door: African American Founding Fathers and Lawyers in Reconstruction South Carolina* (Columbia, S.C., 2000), 130–165.

8. New York *Times*, February 21 and March 18, 1886.

9. Neil Harris, "The Battle for Grant's Tomb," *American Heritage* (August–September 1985), 71–79.

10. James quote in Federal Writers' Project, *New York City Guide*, 288. Original in James, *The American Scene* (New York, 1907), 144.

11. Federal Writers' Project, *New York City Guide: A Comprehensive Guide to the Five Boroughs of the Metropolis* (New York, 1939), 288.

12. New York *Times*, June 18, 1926, documents such a group of Columbia students.

13. New York *Times*, October 8, 2000. Similar criticisms from Harlem residents emerged in discussions with Tom DeMott, a local community activist. Interview, May 20, 2003, in author's possession.

BIBLIOGRAPHY

Manuscript Collections

Butler Library, Columbia University
   John A. Dix Papers
   Kilroe Collection of Tammaniana
   Papers of the Woman Suffrage Association of New York State
Houghton Library, Harvard University
   E. L. Godkin Papers
   Charles Eliot Norton Papers
Library of Congress
   August Belmont Papers
   William Maxwell Evarts Papers
   Horace Greeley Papers
   Frederick Law Olmsted Papers
National Archives
   Letters to the Secretary of War, 1865–1868
New York City Municipal Archives
   Mayors' Papers
New-York Historical Society
   Citizens' Association Records
   Reuben Eaton Fenton Papers
   Horace Greeley Papers
New York Public Library
   Bryant-Godwin Collection
   Committee of Seventy Papers

E. L. Godkin Papers, Miscellaneous Collections
Henry George Papers
Horace Greeley Papers
Josephine Shaw Lowell Miscellaneous Papers
Samuel J. Tilden Papers
New York State Library
    Reuben Eaton Fenton Papers
    Edwin Morgan Collection
    Political Broadsides Collection
    Horatio Seymour Collection
    Emma Waite Diary
Union League Club (New York, N.Y.) Library
    Union League Club Papers

Government Documents

Hoffman, John T. *The Public Papers of John T. Hoffman, 1869–70–71–72.* Albany, N.Y., 1872.

Lowell, Josephine Shaw. *Report on the Subject of Vagrancy.* Albany, N.Y., 1877.

New York (State) Assembly. *Documents of the Assembly of the State of New York; 98th Session—1875.* Albany, N.Y., 1875.

———. *Journal of the Assembly of the State of New York.* Albany, N.Y., 1867.

———. *Journal of the Assembly of the State of New York: At Their Ninety-Sixth Session.* Albany, N.Y., 1873.

New York (State) Board of Charities. *Tenth Annual Report of the State Board of Charities.* Albany, N.Y., 1877.

New York (State) Commission to Devise a Plan for the Government of Cities in the State of New York. "Report of the Commission to Devise a Plan for the Government of Cities in the State of New York Presented to the Legislature, March 6, 1877," in *Documents of the Assembly of the State of New York.* Albany, N.Y., 1877.

New York (State) Constitutional Convention, 1867–1868. *Documents of the Convention of the State of New York, 1867–1868.* Albany, N.Y., 1868.

———. *Journal of the Convention of the State of New York begun and held at the Capitol in the City of Albany, on the 4th Day of June 1867.* Albany, 1867.

———. *Proceedings and Debates of the Constitutional Convention of the State of New York. Held in the City of Albany. Reported by Edward F. Underhill, official reporter.* Albany, N.Y., 1868.

———. *The amended Constitution of the State of New York adopted by the Con-*

vention of 1867–1868 together with the manner and form of submission and an address to the people. Albany, N.Y., 1868.

New York (City) Board of Aldermen. *Documents of the Board of Aldermen of the City of New York.* New York, 1866.

United States Congress. *Congressional Globe.* Washington, D.C., 1866–1871.

Newspapers and Periodicals
(All published in Manhattan unless otherwise indicated)

Advance
Alarm Bell of Liberty
Argus (Albany)
Banner of Liberty
Black Republican and Office Holder's Journal
Boys in Blue
Broome [County] *Republican and Standard* (Binghamton, N.Y.)
Cigar Makers' Official Journal
Citizen
Citizen and Round Table
Colored Citizen (Cincinnati)
Daily News
Evening Post
Frank Leslie's Illustrated Weekly
Freedman (Boston)
Freedman's Journal (Boston)
Freeman's Journal and Catholic Register
Globe
Harper's Weekly
Herald
International Review
Irish American
Irish Citizen
Irish World and American Industrial Liberator
John Swinton's Paper
Journal of Commerce
Labor Standard (New Haven)
Leader
Nation
National Anti-Slavery Standard

National Workman
New Era (Washington, D.C.)
New National Era (Washington, D.C.)
New Yorker Staats-Zeitung
New Yorker Volkszeitung
Niggerhead and Blue Law Advocate
North American Review (Boston)
People's Advocate (Washington, D.C.)
Principia and National Era
Revolution
Toiler
Woodhull and Claflin's Weekly
Workingmen's Advocate

Pamphlets and Broadsides

Butler, William Allen. *Our Great Metropolis: Its Growth, Misgovernment and Needs*. New York, 1880.

Chanler, John W. *This Is a White Workingman's Government*. Washington, D.C., 1866.

Citizens' Association of New York. *The Constitutional Convention. The Metropolitan Commissions, Expenses, etc.* New York, 1867.

———. *The Constitutional Convention. The Basis or General Plan for the Government of the City of New York*. New York, 1867.

———. *Items of Abuse in the Government of the City of New York. Taxpayers, Citizens, Read! Read! Read!* New York, 1866.

Curtis, George William. *Equal Rights for Women: A Speech by George William Curtis in the Constitutional Convention of New York, at Albany, July 19, 1867*. Boston, 1867.

Greeley, Horace. *Letter to a Politician (Samuel J. Tilden)*. Brooklyn, 1877.

Lathers, Col. Richard. *South Carolina, Her Wrongs and the Remedy, Delivered to the Opening of the Taxpayers' Convention in Columbia, S.C., February 17, 1874*. Charleston, 1874.

Lawrence, A. R., Jr. *The Government of Cities*. New York, 1868.

n.a. *Civil Rights: A History of the New York Riot of 1871. The Hibernian Riot and the "Insurrection of the Capitalists." A History of the Important Events in New York, in the Midsummer of 1871*. New York, 1871.

n.a. *National Celebration of Union Victories, March 6, 1865*. New York, 1865.

n.a. *Restoration and Peace! National Union Celebration at Union Square*. New York, 1866.

New York Colored Citizens State Central Committee. *Call for a State Convention, March 1869.*

———. *Petition Presented to the State Constitutional Convention, June 17, 1867.*

Sterne, Simon. *Suffrage in Cities.* New York, 1878.

Swinton, John. *John Swinton's Travels: Current Views and Notes on Forty Days in France and England.* New York, 1880.

———. *The Tompkins Square Outrage.* New York, 1874.

Taxpayers' Association of New York. *Review of the Legislation of 1877.* New York, 1878.

Tilden, Samuel J. *The New York city Ring: its origin, maturity and fall.* New York, 1873.

Workingmen's Party of the United States. *Declaration of Principles of the Workingmen's Party of the United States* (1876), in Philip S. Foner, *The Workingmen's Party of the United States: A History of the First Marxist Party in the Americas,* 115–116. Minneapolis, 1984.

Nineteenth-Century Publications

Adams, Charles Francis, Jr. "The Protection of the Ballot in National Elections," in *Journal of Social Science* 1 (1869), 91–111.

Bellows, Henry C. *Historical Sketch of the Union League Club of New York City: Its Origin, Organization, and Work, 1863–1879.* New York, 1879.

Bigelow, John. *Life of Samuel Jones Tilden.* New York, 1876.

Citizens' Committee. *Obsequies of Abraham Lincoln in Union Square, New York, April 25, 1865.* New York, 1865.

Council of Hygiene and Public Health of the Citizens' Association of New York. *Report of the Council of Hygiene and Public Health of the Citizens' Association of New York Upon the Sanitary Condition of the City.* New York, 1866.

Davenport, John Isaacs. *The Election Frauds of New York City and Their Prevention. Volume I. Eleven Years of Fraud—1860–1870.* New York, 1881.

Fortune, T. Thomas. *Black and White: Land, Labor and Politics in the South.* New York, 1884.

Headley, Joel Tyler. *The Great Riots of New York City, 1712–1873.* New York, 1873.

Hitchcock, Roswell Dwight. *Socialism.* New York, 1879.

James, Henry Ammon. *Communism in America.* New York, 1879.

McNeill, George E. *The Labor Movement: The Problem of Today.* New York, 1887.

National Convention of Colored Men. *Proceedings of the National Convention of Colored Men, Held in Syracuse, New York, October 4–7, 1864.* Boston, 1864.

Prentiss, George L. *Our National Bane; or, The Dry Rot in American Politics. A Tract for the Times Touching Civil Service Reform.* New York, 1877.

Smith, James McCune, ed. *A Memorial Discourse by Henry Highland Garnet.* Philadelphia, 1865.

Sterne, Simon. "The Administration of American Cities," in *The International Review* 4 (1877), 631–646.

Secondary Literature

Amar, Akhil Reed. *The Bill of Rights: Creation and Reconstruction.* New Haven, 1998.

Anbinder, Tyler. *Five Points: The 19th Century New York City Neighborhood That Invented Tap Dance, Stole Elections, and Became the World's Most Notorious Slum.* New York, 2001.

Armstrong, William M., ed. *The Gilded Age Letters of E. L. Godkin.* Albany, N.Y., 1974.

Baker, Jean H. *Affairs of Party: The Political Culture of Northern Democrats in the Mid-Nineteenth Century.* Ithaca, N.Y., 1983.

Barrows, Chester L. *William M. Evarts: Lawyer, Diplomat, Statesman.* Chapel Hill, N.C., 1941.

Beckert, Sven. *The Monied Metropolis: New York City and the Consolidation of the American Bourgeoisie, 1850–1896.* New York, 2001.

Bender, Thomas. *New York Intellect: A History of Intellectual Life in New York City, From 1750 to the Beginnings of Our Own Time.* New York, 1987.

Bensel, Richard Franklin. *Yankee Leviathan: The Origins of Central State Authority in America, 1859–1877.* New York, 1990.

Bernstein, Iver. *The New York City Draft Riots: Their Significance for American Society and Politics in the Age of the Civil War.* New York, 1990.

Blight, David. *Race and Reunion: The Civil War in American Memory.* Cambridge, Mass., 2001.

Burke, Albie. "Federal Regulation of Congressional Elections in Northern Cities, 1871–1894." Ph.D. diss., University of Chicago, 1968.

Burrows, Edwin G., and Mike Wallace. *Gotham: A History of New York City to 1898.* New York, 1999.

Callow, Alexander. *The Tweed Ring.* New York, 1965.

Cohen, Nancy. *The Reconstruction of American Liberalism, 1865–1914.* Chapel Hill, N.C., 2002.

Cohen, Roger A. "The Lost Jubilee: New York Republicans and the Politics of Reconstruction and Reform, 1867–1878." Ph.D. diss., Columbia University, 1975.

Cook, Adrian. *The Armies of the Streets: The New York City Draft Riots of 1863.* Lexington, Ky., 1974.

Dubois, Ellen C. *Feminism and Suffrage: The Emergence of an Independent Women's Movement in America, 1848–1869.* Ithaca, N.Y., 1978.

Du Bois, W.E.B. *Black Reconstruction in America, 1860–1880.* New York, 1935.

Farley, Ena. *The Underside of Reconstruction in New York: The Struggle for Black Equality.* New York, 1993.

Field, Phyllis F. *The Politics of Race in New York: The Struggle for Black Suffrage in the Civil War Era.* Ithaca, N.Y., 1982.

Flick, Alexander C. *Samuel Jones Tilden: A Study in Political Sagacity.* New York, 1939.

Foner, Eric. *Reconstruction: America's Unfinished Revolution, 1863–1877.* New York, 1988.

Foner, Philip S. *The Great Labor Uprising of 1877.* New York, 1977.

———. *The Workingmen's Party of the United States: A History of the First Marxist Party in the Americas.* Minneapolis, 1984.

Foord, John. *The Life and Public Services of Simon Sterne.* London, 1903.

Gellman, David N., and David Quigley, eds. *Jim Crow New York: A Documentary History of Race and Citizenship, 1777–1877.* New York, 2003.

Gillette, William. *Retreat from Reconstruction, 1869–1879.* Baton Rouge, La., 1979.

———. *The Right to Vote: Politics and the Passage of the Fifteenth Amendment.* Baltimore, 1965.

Gordon, Michael A. *The Orange Riots: Irish Political Violence in New York City, 1870 and 1871.* Ithaca, N.Y., 1993.

Grossman, Lawrence. *The Democratic Party and the Negro: Northern and National Politics, 1868–1892.* Urbana, Ill., 1976.

Gutman, Herbert G. "The Tompkins Square 'Riot' in New York City on January 13, 1874: A Reexamination of Its Causes and Aftermath," in *Labor History* 6 (Winter 1965), 48–70.

———. "The Failure of the Movement by the Unemployed for Public Works in 1873," in *Political Science Quarterly* 80 (June 1965), 254–276.

Hammack, David. *Power and Society: Greater New York at the Turn of the Century.* New York, 1982.

Jackson, Kenneth T., ed. *The Encyclopedia of New York City.* New Haven, 1995.

Kaczorowski, Robert. *The Politics of Judicial Interpretation: The Federal Courts, Department of Justice and Civil Rights, 1866–1876.* New York, 1985.

Katz, Philip M. *From Appomattox to Montmartre: Americans and the Paris Commune.* Cambridge, Mass., 1998.

Keller, Morton. *The Art and Politics of Thomas Nast.* New York, 1965.

Keyssar, Alexander. *The Right to Vote: The Contested History of Democracy in the United States.* New York, 2000.

Lincoln, Charles Z. *The Constitutional History of New York from the Beginning of the Colonial Period to the Year 1905, Showing the Origin, Development, and Judicial Construction of the Constitution.* Rochester, N.Y., 1906.

Litwack, Leon. *Been in the Storm So Long: The Aftermath of Slavery.* New York, 1979.

Lorini, Alessandra. *Rituals of Race: American Public Culture and the Search for Racial Democracy.* Charlottesville, Va., 1999.

Mandelbaum, Seymour. *Boss Tweed's New York.* New York, 1965.

McGerr, Michael E. *The Decline of Popular Politics: The American North, 1865–1928.* New York, 1986.

Messer-Kruse, Timothy. *The Yankee International: Marxism and the American Reform Tradition, 1848–1876.* Chapel Hill, N.C., 1998.

Mohr, James C. *The Radical Republicans and Reform in New York During Reconstruction.* Ithaca, N.Y., 1973.

Montgomery, David. *Beyond Equality: Labor and the Radical Republicans, 1862–1872.* New York, 1967.

Mushkat, Jerome. *The Reconstruction of the New York Democracy, 1861–1874.* Rutherford, N.J., 1981.

Nadel, Stanley. *Little Germany: Ethnicity, Religion, and Class in New York City, 1845–1880.* Urbana, Ill., 1990.

Nelson, William E. *The Fourteenth Amendment: From Political Principle to Judicial Doctrine.* Cambridge, Mass., 1988.

Ofari, Earl. *Let Your Motto Be Resistance: The Life and Thought of Henry Highland Garnet.* Boston, 1972.

Polakoff, Keith I. *The Politics of Inertia: The Election of 1876 and the End of Reconstruction.* Baton Rouge, La., 1973.

Richardson, Heather Cox. *The Death of Reconstruction: Race, Labor, and Politics in the Post–Civil War North, 1865–1901.* Cambridge, Mass., 2001.

Rosenberg, Charles E. *The Cholera Years: The United States in 1832, 1849, and 1866.* Chicago, 1962.

Rosenwaike, Ira. *Population History of New York City.* Syracuse, N.Y., 1972.

Rosenzweig, Roy, and Elizabeth Blackmar. *The Park and the People: A History of Central Park.* Ithaca, N.Y., 1992.

Ross, Marc. "John Swinton, Journalist and Reformer: The Active Years, 1857–1887." Ph.D. diss., New York University, 1969.

Ryan, Mary P. *Civic Wars: Democracy and Public Life in the American City During the Nineteenth Century*. Berkeley, 1997.

Schneider, Dorothee. *Trade Unions and Community: The German Working Class in New York City, 1870–1900*. Urbana, Ill., 1994.

Sproat, John G. *"The Best Men": Liberal Reformers in the Gilded Age*. New York, 1968.

Thornbrough, Emma Lou. *T. Thomas Fortune: Militant Journalist*. Chicago, 1972.

Van Deusen, Glyndon G. *Horace Greeley: Nineteenth-Century Crusader*. Philadelphia, 1953.

Vorenberg, Michael. *Final Freedom: The Civil War, the Abolition of Slavery and the Thirteenth Amendment*. New York, 2001.

Waugh, Joan. *Unsentimental Reformer: The Life of Josephine Shaw Lowell*. Cambridge, Mass., 1998.

Wood, Forrest G. *Black Scare: The Racist Response to Emancipation and Reconstruction*. Berkeley, 1968.

ACKNOWLEDGMENTS

On a Friday afternoon in February 1993, I presented the first fragment of what would eventually become *Second Founding* to a seminar of urbanists at New York University. As I was walking home, the beauty of the late winter sky was interrupted by the sound of distant helicopters. The World Trade Center, a passerby on Eighth Street mumbled, had been bombed. Eight years later, after a final summer of research in Manhattan, my junior faculty leave, devoted to completing this book, began at my word processor on the morning of Monday, September 10, 2001. For the next days and months, this book was completed as New York's relation to the rest of America was again remade.

At long last, I can offer thanks to the many individuals who have offered assistance over the past decade. Librarians and archivists were essential guides at a range of institutions: the New York State Library, Houghton and Widener Libraries at Harvard University, Bobst Library at N.Y.U., O'Neill Library at Boston College, the New York Public Library, the New-York Historical Society, the private library of the Manhattan

Union League Club, New York City's Muncipal Archives, the Library of Congress, and the National Archives. Fellowships from Amherst College and New York University carried me through the early stages of research. A Charlotte Newcombe Dissertation Fellowship enabled the completion of the original dissertation. Boston College and the Gilder-Lehrman Institute of American History funded last-minute research and final revisions. At Hill & Wang, I've been lucky to work with both Elisabeth Sifton and Thomas LeBien. Their assistants—Nina Pesut, Danny Mulligan, and Kristy McGowan—helped guide this first-time author through the publishing process.

A number of scholars have been generous with ideas along the way. Comments from Daniel Goodwin, Martin Crawford, Sven Beckert, Richard Schneirov, Timothy Messer-Kruse, David Brion Davis, Thelma Foote, Jay Fliegelman, and J. Morgan Kousser all helped in developing this book's arguments. *New York History* published a version of chapter five, while *American Nineteenth-Century History* published portions of chapters seven and eight. In graduate school, I learned from the examples of David Reimers, Molly Nolan, Martha Hodes, Susan Ware, Saverio Giovacchini, Valentijn Byvanck, Amy Richter, Michael Lerner, and John Baick. In particular, Ira Katznelson and Liz Cohen helped deepen my engagement with the complex political cultures of urban America.

A few friends of longer standing helped me through my Reconstruction years. Paul Babbitt has lent his ear to my ideas—good and bad—since middle school. Dave Gellman, my collaborator in the wards of antebellum Manhattan, has shared the joys and frustrations of academic life with me since our undergraduate days. Neil Sullivan and Jim Perkins were ideal general readers of early versions of chapter eight. Todd and Holly Lyons, Paul Schwartzberg and Lisa Waldman, and

Maryellen O'Connor kindly hosted me on various research trips along the eastern seaboard. The DeMott family has welcomed me for almost two decades now. At Boston College, I owe thanks to newer friends who have been generous with their support. I've learned a great deal about the practice of history working alongside my colleagues in the History Department. Lynn Lyerly and Kevin Kenny merit special thanks for their close readings of the entire manuscript.

My greatest intellectual debt lies with my teachers. Margaret Richardson and Robert Moir brought history to life in their classrooms. In college, David Wills patiently put up with a somewhat unreliable thesis advisee. Bob Gross remains the ideal undergraduate mentor, in my mind's eye and for so many of his former students. In 1991, I moved from the public schools of Brooklyn to the N.Y.U. History Department and quickly found a home as a Tom Bender student. Two years later, this project began with a phone call from Tom, mentioning a footnote he'd found on something called the Tilden Commission. So much in the past decade I owe to Tom's unfailing generosity. This book is a first attempt to repay Tom for many things, not least his commitment to the historian's larger, public obligations.

The Quigley and Iossa families provided the foundation for this project over many decades. Vincent Iossa, my grandfather and an immigrant from southern Italy, died in the early stages of research. His stories of immigrant New York in the early twentieth century have long been the foundation of my historical imagination. My sisters Ellen and Ann and I have shared a common love of the past, dating back to our countless childhood trips from New York to historic sites up and down the eastern seaboard. Ann deserves special thanks for her more recent assistance, both financial and automotive. My parents, Lucille and Patrick Quigley, have believed in me for almost four decades now. For that belief, and for so much more, I thank them.

Nathaniel has grown up with this project and now looks forward to reading it. His younger brother Tyrone has only lately come to know of this book's existence, but that hasn't stopped him from celebrating its impending completion. And baby Graham arrived just in time for the page proofs. The boys have sustained me with their wide-eyed curiosity. Through it all, from Amherst to Brooklyn to Cambridge, Megan DeMott-Quigley has been my world.

Cambridge, Mass.
October 2003

INDEX